IS THE ANTICHRIST ALIVE TODAY?

Unless otherwise specified, all Scriptures are taken from the King James Version of the Holy Bible.

IS THE ANTICHRIST ALIVE TODAY?
© 2011 by Dr. N. W. Hutchings

All rights reserved under International Copyright Law. No part of this book may be used or reproduced in any manner whatsoever without written permission of the publisher, except in the case of brief quotations in articles and reviews. For more information write: Bible Belt Publishing, 500 Beacon Dr., Oklahoma City, OK 73127, (800) 652-1144, *www.swrc.com*.

Printed in the United States of America

ISBN 1-933641-43-6

IS THE ANTICHRIST ALIVE TODAY?

Dr. Noah Hutchings

Table of Contents

Chapter 1
  The Enemy and the Enmity 7

Chapter 2
  The Spirit of Iniquity 21

Chapter 3
  The Son of Perdition 43

Chapter 4
  Influence of Antichrist on Today's Ecology 53

Chapter 5
  Influence of Antichrist on Today's Economy 64

Chapter 6
  Economic Agents of Antichrist 77

Chapter 7
  Spirit of Antichrist in Today's Church. 85

Chapter 8
  Antichrist Influence in Nations Today 101

Chapter 9
  The Antichrist System 114

Chapter 10
  Antichrist—His Name and Nature. 125

Chapter 11
  666 and Counting 138

Chapter 12
  What Does 666 Mean to You?. 152

Chapter 13
  Is the Antichrist Alive Today?. 165

Chapter 1

The Enemy and the Enmity

The rebellion which divided the Kingdom of God into two opposing and warring kingdoms began way back in the eons of time. Although the Bible draws aside the curtain of the past to give us only brief glimpses of this catastrophic event, we are assured in the Scriptures that it did occur when a prince in the government of God decided to exalt his provincial throne above the Throne of God (Isaiah 14:12-13). In the continuing struggle between God and the rebel, identified as Lucifer who became Satan (the enemy of God), the Evil One has placed his own fallen angelic rulers over certain heavenly planets that have been occupied by his forces (Ezekiel 28:18; Ephesians 6:12; Revelation 12:7-8). According to the tenth chapter of Daniel, Satan has his own angelic rulers whom he has appointed to rule the nations in preparation for that day when he will be able to crown his man as the king of planet Earth, thereby forever laying claim to the world as a part of his kingdom of evil.

As far as man and this earth are concerned, the beginning of the story of Christ (God's Savior) versus Antichrist (Satan's earthly king) is related in Genesis 3:14-15:

And the Lord God said unto the serpent, Because thou hast done this, thou art cursed above all cattle, and above every beast of the field; upon thy belly shalt thou go, and dust shalt thou eat all the days of thy life: And I will put enmity between thee and the woman, and between thy seed and her seed; it shall bruise thy head, and thou shalt bruise his heel.

We have no difficulty in presenting a great host of Bible scholars who readily agree that the "seed of woman" refers to the Savior of mankind, the Lord Jesus Christ, who was born of a virgin without the agency of a human father, the Son of God who was conceived by the Holy Spirit to become incarnate in a body of human flesh. Without such a promise from God, there would have been no reason for continuing the history of man beyond the Garden of Eden. Without a Redeemer to save the human race from the catastrophe of sin, man would have been condemned eternally to exist in misery, despair, hopelessness, and perdition until God put him out of his misery or man destroyed himself. This was Satan's plan when he led Adam and Eve to transgress against the Creator in the Garden of Eden, and naturally the Evil One would oppose the purpose of God to save man through a promised Deliverer.

But now we come to another personality mentioned by God in Genesis 3:15, and this person is referred to as "thy seed," relating back to the serpent, or the devil. In other words, as the consequence of Eve being beguiled by Satan, two separate and distinct personalities would be born—the seed of the woman, and the seed of the serpent. We notice also in Genesis 3:15 that permanent relationships were established by God between the four parties directly concerned in man's fall. The four parties mentioned are the woman, the serpent, the promised seed of woman, and the promised seed of the serpent. The relationship established by God among the four parties was:

1. There would be enmity between the serpent and the woman.
2. There would be enmity between the seed of woman and the seed of the serpent.

The root word for enmity is the same as that for enemy. Enmity means a continuing feeling of mistrust, antagonism, bitterness, and hatred that keeps two parties at cross purposes with each other. Thus, we see from the beginning of our Bible that two personalities would come upon the world scene: one would be the Savior, the Christ, and one would be the Destroyer, the Antichrist. One would save that which God created in His own image, and one would attempt to complete the destruction that Satan began. One would be dedicated to carrying out the plan and purpose of God for man; the other would be just as dedicated to carrying out the devil's program of chaos and destruction. One would be consecrated to restoring the planet Earth to the Kingdom of God; the other would be consecrated to ruling the Earth for Satan. The countdown for Antichrist was begun in Genesis 3:15.

The enmity that God placed between the woman and Satan began to manifest itself with the birth of Cain and Abel. We read in 1 John 3:12 that Cain was of that wicked one, meaning Satan, and he killed his righteous brother. For all practical purposes, this evil deed of Cain would have ended the human race had not God given Adam and Eve other children. If such had been the case, Cain would have been the Antichrist, and the devil would have won the battle for this Earth. However, God gave to Adam and Eve other sons and daughters, and Cain was left behind in the history of this spiritual warfare between God and the devil over the salvation of the human race. Therefore, Cain was only a type of the coming man of sin, and not a fulfillment of the prophecy of the seed of the serpent declared in Genesis 3:15.

The attempt by Satan to make Cain the Antichrist is evident in the wicked deeds of Eve's firstborn son. We read in Genesis 4:4–5,8:

> And Abel, he also brought of the firstlings of his flock and of the fat thereof. And the LORD had respect unto Abel and to his offering: But unto Cain and to his offering he had not respect. And Cain was very wroth, and his countenance fell.... And Cain talked with Abel his brother: and it came to pass, when they were in the field, that Cain rose up against Abel his brother, and slew him.

The apostle John tells us much about the Antichrist in his first epistle, and in 1 John 3:12 we read, "Not as Cain, who was of that wicked one, and slew his brother...." The Apostle Paul used almost the exact terminology in reference to the Antichrist in 2 Thessalonians 2:7–8. Certainly, Cain was a forerunner of this wicked and devil-controlled person. Abel offered a blood sacrifice, a type of the atoning work of Christ on the cross, and for this reason Cain killed him. Cain was actually rebelling against God's plan for bringing forth the seed of woman, the Savior.

He had enmity in his heart against the promised Christ. We should note that God not only had no respect for Cain's offering, He had no respect for Cain as a person.

Cain was also a type of antichrist in other ways. God gave him a mark, and we read in Revelation 13:17 that the Antichrist will have his own mark. We find another identifying mark of Antichrist in Cain in Genesis 4:17: "... and he builded a city...." It has been the desire of every forerunner of Antichrist to build a great city, and there is much more involved here than just a center for trade and commerce. Every foretype of Antichrist has raised up a city upon which the carnal, the unregenerate children of the devil, can fix their affections and devotions. Thus, they will be kept from looking for another city, the heavenly Jerusalem, the dwelling place that God has prepared for those who will inherit eternal life through faith in Christ, God's only begotten Son.

The fact that Cain built a city, which doubtless included his family and followers, would also seem to indicate that others also must have built cities. Anyone today can Google "cities on the ocean floor" and see actual pictures and descriptions of cities that once existed that are now on the ocean floors. According to Ussher, it was December 7, 2349 B.C., that God commanded Noah to enter the Ark. This would mean that from the creation of Adam and Eve to the Flood would have been a time period of about sixteen hundred and fifty years, sufficient time for mankind to multiply and build cities on every landmass of the earth, as indicated in Scripture. However, nothing will be found in school books about these cities, as they would not fit into the absurd evolutionary theory taught by law in the public school systems of our nation.

The trail of enmity between Satan and the woman, the seed of woman and the seed of the serpent, continued from Cain down through man's history. The fallen angelic invasion of Genesis 6:2 was an attempt by the devil to corrupt the entire human race whereby no woman could give birth to the Savior. But there was one man, Noah, who was found to be perfect in that generation. He alone remained free of this alien blood contamination.

According to Genesis 6, as referenced in other related scriptures, sons of God married the daughters of men, and the result of such ungodly unions resulted in a race of giants. Many believe the "sons of God" were descendants of Seth who married the daughters, or descendants, of Cain. In any event, the Septuagint interprets the Hebrew text as angels of God; so did Josephus (*Antiquities,* 3:1); and so did Apollos. These angelic offspring are referenced in the Hebrew text as Nephilim. Good men marrying bad women, or vice versa, has never produced a race of giants, so it is obvious that the "sons of God" of Genesis 6 were rebellious angels who left their created order (first estate) to corrupt God's creation at Satan's command (2 Peter 2:4; Jude 6). The account in Genesis 6 indicates the Nephilim were those beings described in Greek mythology. Giants are also characters in children's fairy tales. The giants of antiquity are mentioned also in English, French, German, and other ancient literature accounts. William Cody (Buffalo Bill) noted in his autobiography that the Pawnee Indians' ancestors had to contend with giants three times the height of average men.

God brought Noah and his household through the judgment that destroyed the devil-contaminated antediluvian generation of man, and established a new dispensation whereby His plan and purpose for man and this world could continue. But once again Satan brought forth his man to act at cross-purposes, or against God's redemptive program. The name of the devil's man in that particular time and situation was Nimrod, and we read about him in Genesis 10:9–10: "He was a mighty hunter before the LORD: wherefore it is said, Even as Nimrod the mighty hunter before the LORD. And the beginning of his kingdom was Babel...." Nimrod was led by Satan to formulate a counterplan that would be at cross-purposes to the will of God for that dispensation. And God's will was that mankind should be divided into races and nations within the framework of human government whereby men could freely seek God and come to a knowledge of the truth and be saved. God instructed the human race to do one thing, but Nimrod told them to do quite the opposite, and his counterprogram is outlined in Genesis 11:4: "And they said, Go to, let us build us a city and a tower, whose top may reach unto heaven; and let us make us a name, lest we be scattered abroad upon the face of the whole earth."

On leading tours to Turkey, we often pass through the old area of Galatia where there are hundreds of mounts from fifty to three hundred feet high. The area is called "the land of giants," where road construction has uncovered the skeletons of giants from fourteen to seventeen feet tall. At Glen Rose, Texas, and other sites in Texas, footprints two feet long have been found preserved in stone. In Central and South America, human skulls three sizes larger than average adult skulls have been found. All the above information can be verified on documented Internet sources.

It is evident from this antediluvian account in Scripture, as verified by documented ancient sources, that the sons of God were angels sent by Satan to corrupt mankind and take over the planet Earth. We read that only Noah was perfect in his generation, meaning that only he and his family had escaped this satanic DNA corruption. It also appears that much of the animal kingdom had been contaminated, as Noah was commanded to take "clean beasts" into the Ark by sevens, and "unclean beasts" by twos (Genesis 7:2). This could explain why there are no dinosaurs in the world today.

The reason for God dividing mankind into races and establishing them within the bounds of nations is made known in Acts 17:26–27: "[God] hath made of one blood all nations of men for to dwell on all the face of the earth, and hath determined the times before appointed, and the bounds of their habitation; That they should seek the Lord, if haply they might feel after him, and find him, though he be not far from every one of us." This is the same truth enlarged upon in 1 Timothy 2:1–6.

Nimrod was a mighty hunter of the souls of men, and he sought to ensnare the entire human race into his kingdom, Babel. Nimrod's program was antichrist in that he attempted to prevent the divisions of the world into nations whereby men of all races could come to the knowledge that there is one mediator between God and man, the Lord Jesus Christ. Nimrod was also a type of the Antichrist, in that he worked to prevent a kingdom of nations here upon earth to be ruled over by the King of Kings, the Lord Jesus Christ, at His Second Coming. He set himself at cross-purposes with God.

According to Assyrian history, Nimrod was a great king

who founded two great cities—Babylon and Nineveh. Ussher places the Tower of Babel at 2242 B.C., which would be soon after the Flood and the birth of Peleg, in whose days we read the earth was divided. It is thought that before the Flood, all the landmass of the planet was on one continent. If the dividing of the earth meant a separation of the landmass into continents and islands, this would help explain why Nimrod would have ordered the building of the Tower of Babel. Nimrod, a grandson of Ham, thought to keep all the world under his authority, the same ambition of the coming Antichrist. We might also wonder if the Antichrist will not also be a descendant of Ham.

However, God confounded the language where the builders of the Tower of Babel could not communicate, and nations evolved according to God's plan, separated by languages, oceans, mountains, color, and other factors. Today, we have instant international communications, the United Nations, and rapid transportation erasing God's guidelines for the separation of nations. All these factors are providing the means for another world ruler of the order of Nimrod to impose his will and laws upon all the world. But we read in Isaiah 30:25–27 that the one-world tower that mankind is building today will fall, just as the Tower of Babel did.

The first type of Antichrist, Cain, had his own religion, but it was a religion of Satan that led him further from his Creator; and likewise, Nimrod imitated his own form of devil worship. Quoting from page 140 of *Dispensational Truth* by Clarence Larkin:

> Babel, or Babylon, was built by Nimrod. Genesis 10:8–10. It was the seat of the first great apostasy. Here the Babylonian

cult was invented, a system claiming to possess the highest wisdom and to reveal the divinest secrets. Before a member could be initiated he had to confess to the priest. . . . Once admitted into this order, men were no longer Babylonians, Assyrians, or Egyptians, but members of a mystical brotherhood, over whom was placed a pontiff or high priest whose word was law.

From the dispensation of human government, we advance to the dispensation of promise and find God's chosen people, Israel, in bondage in Egypt to a cruel and heartless ruler called the Pharaoh. When men fail to accept the mercy and grace of God which are offered in a particular way, God brings an end to that special ministry and ushers in a new dispensation. The dispensation of innocence ended with the death sentence being placed upon Adam and Eve. The dispensation of conscience ended with the Flood. The dispensation of human government, though continuing after Babel on a conditional basis, was ended as the sole and unique hope of the world with the fall of Nimrod's one-world empire. Next, God would have one race of people, the Hebrews, to establish a nation in which all other nations would be blessed and led into the light of God's truth, whereby the planet Earth might be restored to the Kingdom of God. The Hebrew people had by faith accepted God's promise of a nation of holy people leading all men to the truth of the Lord whereby they might be saved. But the Pharaoh stood at cross-purposes with God in His plan and purpose, and he would not allow the children of Israel to return to the land that God had given them so that they could begin carrying out the program of the Lord for that dispensation. The Pharaoh was antichrist, in that he stood in the way of the Hebrew people ultimately bringing forth the Messiah, the King of Kings and Lord of Lords. And what did the Pharaoh have the children of Israel doing while they were in bondage? We read in Exodus 1:11 that they were building great cities. So intent was the devil's man for that hour in filling the world with cities, pyramids, and monuments of stone, that it required ten severe judgments from God before the children of Israel were able to escape. These ten judgments are typical of the ones which the two witnesses of God will bring against the kingdom of Antichrist during the Tribulation (Revelation 11).

The next striking world figure to appear who opposed the bringing in of the Kingdom of God on earth was King Nebuchadnezzar. This gentile ruler built a mighty city of which the hanging gardens, the pseudo-paradise of God, has been listed among the seven wonders of the ancient world. Nebuchadnezzar invaded Judah, destroyed the Lord's House in Jerusalem, and brought the nation under a state of captivity that lasted for seventy years. Although Nebuchadnezzar was brought to an understanding of the reality and power of God in his later years, his early life was committed to opposing God's will for men and nations.

From the dispensation of the law, we advance to the dispensation of grace, and Satan found a likely candidate for his antichrist again to oppose God's program of salvation in the person of Nero, emperor of Rome. Nero possessed an evil and wicked nature even as a child. He murdered members of his own family to gain the throne, including his mother and his wife. He was crowned king of the Roman Empire in A.D. 54, the same year that Paul wrote to the church at Thessalonica,

"For the mystery of iniquity doth already work . . ." (2 Thessalonians 2:7). Satan had two witnesses of God to oppose at this time—the church and Israel. Although Satan had his own men among the Jews to betray and kill Messiah, both that nation and the church had to be destroyed before all the world could worship his man in Rome as God. Nero subsequently issued an edict for the extermination of every Christian, and he sent reinforcements to the Roman military force in Judah to destroy the city and the people. Nero, like all strong types of antichrist, planned to build a great city. He burned Rome, blamed the deed on the Christians, and then revealed plans to build it as an eternal city of his kingdom.

The first epistle of Peter was written to the Jews who had become Christians, and for one reason or another, possibly to escape persecution, had migrated to what is now present-day Turkey, in an area from the Mediterranean coastal region to Ankara in east central Turkey. Peter indicated he was in Babylon at the time. Some contend that he really was in Rome, but this is only an assumption and I see no reason to doubt that he was in Babylon. His second epistle was written to the same congregation as his first epistle (2 Peter 3:1), but probably five or six years later. Whether or not Peter was still in Babylon is not indicated. However, it is indicated in his second epistle that he was probably in prison and was soon to be crucified (2 Peter 1:14). Crucifixion was the favorite form of execution by the Romans for non-Romans. One historical note reported that the Romans had cut down all the trees in Jerusalem for crosses. Nero crucified Christians in Rome, covered them with tar, and burned them to lighten the streets at night.

Paul had appealed his sentence to Nero, which was his

right as he was a Roman citizen. It appears that Paul did appear before Nero, but was sentenced to die by beheading, according to traditional accounts (2 Timothy 4:6). It may be of importance to note that Paul, God's appointed apostle to the gentiles, was beheaded under orders of Nero. The Antichrist will use beheading as his method of execution for Christians who have been saved during the Tribulation (Revelation 20:4). Some theologians believe the Antichrist will be someone from the past whom the devil will bring forth to be the Antichrist. Of course, if this were true, then Nero would be a good candidate.

But like all former types of antichrist, Nero was not quite successful, as God intervened to save the church and a remnant of the Hebrew race. Daniel, Jesus Christ, and the Apostle Paul prophesied that at the end of the age when the fullness of the gentiles was approaching and the Jews began returning to Israel, Satan would again activate his program to place his own false christ in the Temple and exalt his throne above the throne of God.

Christians today are indeed naïve if they believe they will escape the wrath of the gathering storm, because everything that is of God must either be crushed, or removed by God in the Rapture, before the wicked one will make himself known to the world. The Antichrist will be at enmity with everything that is of God, and he will oppose and try to kill everyone who worships God. Like Cain, Nimrod, Pharaoh, Nebuchadnezzar, and Nero, he will promise men a heaven on earth, but, instead, will give them death, suffering, and damnation. According to the signs of the times, we believe he is in the world today. Have you, dear reader, believed the Gospel that you might be saved? The Bible says in John 3:16: "For God so loved the world, that he gave his only begotten Son, that whosoever believeth in him should not perish, but have everlasting life."

Chapter 2

The Spirit of Iniquity

After the passing of Nebuchadnezzar, king of Babylon, from the world scene, no other strong type of antichrist is described in Old Testament scripture. Antiochus Epiphanes (manifestation of the gods), a Greek by race and an Assyrian by nationality, was a type of the coming destroyer and desecrator of the Temple, but his exploits are not recorded in the Bible. Josephus even concluded that Antiochus Epiphanes committed the "abomination of desolation" prophesied by Daniel (Daniel 11:31), when the Assyrian erected an altar to Zeus in the Temple, and offered a swine to his god upon it. However, Josephus was wrong, because Jesus said that the "abomination of desolation" prophesied by Daniel was yet in the future.

The Antichrist is not solely a New Testament revelation. His coming into the world is foretold from Genesis 3:15 (the seed of the serpent, the devil). In the Old Testament the Antichrist is called the "little horn," "the blasphemer," "the Assyrian," and many other names.

Jesus affirmed that the Antichrist would present himself to Israel as the messiah when He said in John 5:43, "I am come in my Father's name, and ye receive me not: if another shall come in his own name, him ye will receive."

Paul in Romans 11 stated that blindness in part had happened to Israel until the fullness of the gentiles be completed. Since Israel rejected Jesus Christ in A.D. 33, the Jews have been looking for another messiah. On leading my fifty-fourth tour to Israel in November 2011, I found that 99.8 percent of Israel still rejects Jesus Christ as the Messiah. Only one in five hundred Israeli Jews believe that Jesus Christ is their Messiah. An Israeli National News release, however, dated November 23, 2011, reports that religious Jews now believe the coming of their Messiah is very near:

> A medieval Jewish prophecy regarding the coming of Israel's Messiah appears to correspond to the current situation in the Middle East, Israel National News reported at the weekend.
>
> A piece of rabbinic literature known as the Yalkut Shimoni touches on many future scenarios both for the nation of Israel and for the world. In its section on the biblical Book of Isaiah and the prophecies contained therein, a rabbi cited by the Yalkut Shimoni states:
>
> "In the year in which the Messiah-King appears, all the nations of the world are provoking each other. The King of Persia provokes an Arab king and the Arab king turns to Aram for advice."
>
> That description closely mirrors Iran's defiant nuclear program and the tension it is creating with Arab states, particularly Saudi Arabia. But what happens next? According to the Yalkut Shimoni:
>
> "The King of Persia goes back and destroys the entire world. And all the nations of the world are in panic and distress and they fall upon their faces and are seized with pains

like those of a woman giving birth...."

A recent report by the International Atomic Energy Agency (IAEA) confirmed that Iran is working on nuclear weapons and that it could probably field such weapons in no more than a year's time. That means diplomatic efforts have failed, and barring a dangerous preemptive strike by Israel and/or America, Iran will obtain nuclear weapons.

Many in the West are now focusing their efforts on downplaying the dangers of a nuclear Iran. They argue that just as the Soviet Union did not use its nuclear weapons against the West, so, too, will Iran show restraint. But such commentaries fail to take into account the deeply ingrained religious ideology of those who rule Iran, who see themselves as the instruments of Allah in ushering in a new golden age for Islam.

What does all this mean for Israel, assuming the Yalkut Shimoni is accurate? The text reads:

"... and Israel are in panic and distress and asking 'where shall we go? Where shall we go?,' and He says to them 'my sons, do not fear; all that I have done, I have done only for you. Why are you afraid? Do not fear, your time of redemption has come, and the final redemption is not like the first redemption, because the first redemption was followed by sorrow and servitude under other kingdoms, but the final redemption is not followed by sorrow and servitude under other kingdoms."

Israel is indeed already showing signs of that panic and distress. Over the past month, Israel has been engaged in tense public debate over whether or not to strike Iran's nuclear facilities, and newspaper spreads have detailed what could happen to the Jewish state both if it attacks and if it does not. Meanwhile, Israel's Home Front Command has been practicing for a massive unconventional missile barrage on Tel Aviv.

It is not known who exactly compiled the Yalkut Shimoni, but the oldest surviving copy dates to around A.D. 1310. Many of the rabbis quoted in the Yalkut Shimoni lived far earlier, during the Talmudic era in the first and second centuries A.D.

On November 15, 2011, Ahmadinejad, Iran's strong man, declared to the world that "these are the last days" and the coming of the Muslim Mahdi was at hand. According to Muslim prophecy, the Mahdi will come and kill everyone in the world who is not a Muslim, and only Muslims will survive to be given the earth.

Paul instructed the early Christians concerning the coming of Antichrist (2 Thessalonians 2). It was possibly the writings of Paul on the Antichrist that the Apostle John later alluded to in A.D. 90, when he wrote in 1 John 4:3: "And every spirit that confesseth not that Jesus Christ is come in the flesh is not of God: and this is that spirit of antichrist, whereof ye have heard that it should come; and even now already is it in the world."

We can conclude from the preceding scripture that although the Antichrist as a person was not in the world in A.D. 90, he must have been somewhere because it was by his spirit that men were denying that Jesus Christ had come in the flesh. As we shall see later, the Antichrist will deny the birth of Jesus Christ up to the very day that he meets the true Messiah at the Battle of Armageddon. Let us keep in mind that the denial of the first advent of Jesus Christ, conceived by the Holy Spirit and born of a virgin, is the identifying trademark of Antichrist.

It is generally agreed by most Bible chronologists that the Epistle of James was the first book of the New Testament to be written (about A.D. 45). The second and third books, in chronological order, are the two epistles of Paul to the Thessalonians (both written in A.D. 54). James, in A.D. 45, referred to the Second Coming of Jesus Christ as an imminent promise (James 5:8). Likewise, Paul wrote to the church at Thessalonica that the return of God's Son from Heaven was a present hope (1 Thessalonians 1:9-10). As long as the Temple was standing in Jerusalem, and as long as there was an opportunity for Israel to repent, recognize the crucified One as the Messiah, and call out for God to send Jesus back, the return of the Lord remained a literal hope (Acts 3:19-20). However, after Paul was arrested by the priesthood, and the elders of Israel rejected the claims presented by Paul from prison concerning Jesus the Christ, the Kingdom door to Israel was shut (Acts 28:28). The fulfillment of the prophecies of Jesus in Matthew 23 concerning the destruction of Jerusalem and the Temple, and the setting aside of Israel, were only a matter of time. It all came to pass in A.D. 70, as secular history abundantly records. Nevertheless, it is of much importance for those Christians who seek to "rightly divide the word of truth," that from the time of Paul's prison declaration to Israel recorded in Acts 28:27-28, the apostle never referred to the return of Christ as a present hope in his lifetime. Thereafter, Paul spoke not of Christ's coming to take him to Heaven in the translation of the church (Rapture), but rather of his departure from this life, through bodily death, to go to be with the Lord (Philippians 1:21–26). Henceforth, after Acts 28:28, Paul placed the setting for the return of Christ in the latter times, or last days. The epistles written by Paul after Acts 28:28 are Ephesians, Philippians, Colossians, 1 Timothy, 2 Timothy, and Titus (Philemon excluded). Only when Jews began to return to the land of Palestine, and Israel was refounded as a nation, could Christians look for the coming of Jesus Christ to consummate the blessed union prophesied in 1 Thessalonians 4:13–18. We are now living in the time when the return of Jesus Christ is an immediate prospect. The importance of this evident truth to our study is that the appearance of Antichrist is to come immediately after the catching away of the church in the air, followed by the Antichrist's seven-year reign over the world, which is to be terminated by the return of Christ to earth with His saints (Revelation 19).

But let us return to the year A.D. 54 and see if we can determine the most important sign referred to by Paul that must appear before the Antichrist can be revealed.

> Now we beseech you, brethren, by the coming of our Lord Jesus Christ, and by our gathering together unto him, That ye be not soon shaken in mind, or be troubled, neither by spirit, nor by word, nor by letter as from us, as that the day of Christ is at hand. Let no man deceive you by any means: for that day shall not come, except there come a falling away first, and that man of sin be revealed, the son of perdition.
> —2 Thessalonians 2:1–3

In analyzing the clues given by Paul concerning the identity and nature of Antichrist, we notice first that the apostle said there must come a falling away first, before such a hideous beast, a man so completely possessed by sin, could be revealed and accepted by the nations as their god. Now by falling away, was Paul speaking only of the membership of the church, or of mankind in general? In considering this question, we point out that the apostle spoke of a "falling away" in two separate epistles. The second reference to "falling away" is found in 1 Timothy 4:1: "Now the Spirit speaketh expressly, that in the latter times some shall **depart from the faith,** giving heed to seducing spirits, and doctrines of devils."

In the reference to the falling away in 1 Timothy 4:1, Paul unquestionably meant the end-time apostasy within the visible church, because he spoke of those who would be deceived by false doctrines and commit abominations in the name of religion. In the first reference to "falling away" in 2 Thessalonians, the apostle spoke of both the apostate church and the unchurched mass, the billions who would be deceived and subsequently damned for worshipping Antichrist as a god and receiving his mark. Thus, the true Christians must be taken out of the world first, as indicated in 2 Thessalonians 2:7, and the minds of the unregenerate be so corrupted that the vast majority will accept this evil and wicked man as the lord and king of planet Earth. This twofold falling away has been in progress for several years. Statistics relating to the crimes of robbery, rape, theft, larceny, and murder have become so enormous that, like the national debt, they have no real meaning to the individual. The only thing concerning the crime rate that means anything to the individual is that, according to the latest statistics, he has one chance in eight during the current year to be robbed, assaulted, be a victim of burglary, be murdered, or raped.

Very seldom are infidelity and divorce condemned from the pulpit. In 1900, there was one divorce in twelve marriages. In 1967, there was one divorce in 3.7 marriages, and the percentages of marriages which endure have steadily declined since 1967. Our local paper, *The Daily Oklahoman*, reported the number of marriages in 1975 in relation to the number of divorces. In Oklahoma City in 1975, there were sixty-seven hundred marriages, but over eight thousand divorces. Divorces exceeded marriages by about twenty-five percent, and this percentage relates to most other metropolitan areas. The 1984 edition of *The World Almanac* reported that for 1982, on a nationwide basis, there were 2,495,000 marriages, and 1,180,000 divorces.

These statistics indicate: (1) the continuing breakup of the family unit; (2) there are more dependent children on welfare rolls; (3) divorce has become so common that the marriage union has no meaning any more; and (4) many couples no longer bother to get a marriage license and take the vows. They simply are taking up housekeeping with no strings attached.

The majority of housewives who do not work, daily watch a parade of television soap operas which glorify fornication, adultery, and alcoholism. Millions of American women shed tears over some television actress who has to go next door to get her sexual satisfaction from her handsome neighbor. Most family television shows, with rare exceptions, continually present a series of situations, or comic dialogue, based on sex and infidelity. In addition, most prime-time television movies are presented within a setting that would have shocked a prostitute fifty years ago. For example, one television movie was based on the antics of an airline stewardess who had one husband in the United States and another in England and the movie berated the intemperance of both men when they objected to the poor dear's efforts to keep them both happy. Another television movie, shown from eight to ten p.m., available for viewing by most children, was based on the life of a woman who lived with a man for a month, and then with another man the following month. She had a different man for each month of the year, and this movie brought out that it was so wonderful that this woman could touch so many lives.

As we consider that condition of our nation today in its worldwide setting, we understand how Lot must have felt, and we are informed in Luke 17 of Jesus' warning that as it was in the days of Noah and the days of Lot, so it would be when He comes again. In perusing the *2011 World Almanac* we find:

» In 1932, thirteen out of seventy-nine marriages ended in divorce.
» In 2010, thirty-four out of sixty-six marriages ended in divorce, more than half.
» In the past sixteen years 80 million babies have been born.
» More than 50 percent of the 80 million were born out of wedlock.
» In the past sixteen years there were 22 million recorded abortions.
» In 1962 it became illegal to pray or read the Bible in public schools.
» It is now illegal to openly criticize or disagree with the homosexual lifestyle.

- » President Obama declared June to be Gay Pride month.
- » President Obama said that homosexuals are better than heterosexuals.
- » President Obama has appointed over 150 homosexuals to high positions.
- » This past month the flag of Sodom flew over the Federal Reserve; tomorrow, the White House?
- » The United States, under the blessing of God, is the richest nation the world has ever known, yet our money is supporting pagan nations around the world. We are hopelessly in debt and most of what we eat, wear, or sit on has to be imported.
- » We have an illegal alien problem that our government doesn't care enough about to solve; our prisons are overcrowded, and the inmates are mostly from one-parent homes.

In Israel God called men like Elijah and Jeremiah to warn the nation of their sins and call for repentance. On two occasions kings Asa and Josiah tore down the bathhouses and chased the sodomites out of Jerusalem, and in turn God blessed Israel.

Where are the pastors who are calling our nation, including its leaders, to give an account for our sins nationally, individually, and collectively? We do thank God for every faithful pastor, but too many have forgotten the responsibility of their calling; too comfortable in their church-provided, rent-free homes; too entertained while cruising in their Cadillacs. To use a 501(c)3 status as an excuse for not speaking out against the wicked generation of our day, including wickedness in high places, is cowardice.

Jesus said in Matthew 24:37, "But as the days of Noe were, so shall also the coming of the Son of man be." Of the generation that was destroyed in the Flood, we read in Genesis 6:5: "And GOD saw that the wickedness of man was great in the earth, and that every imagination of the thoughts of his heart was only evil continually."

Of the wicked condition of the antediluvians, Paul wrote in Romans 1:26–27:

> For this cause God gave them up unto vile affections: for even their women did change the natural use into that which is against nature: And likewise also the men, leaving the natural use of the woman, burned in their lust one toward another; men with men working that which is unseemly, and receiving in themselves that recompence of their error which was meet.

Today in our own nation, the Mattachine Society reports that at least one in ten Americans is a homosexual. One newspaper in San Francisco reported there were seventy thousand known couples living in a homosexual relationship in that city alone. England has repealed all laws restricting sexual perversion because of the great increase in homosexuals in that country.

There is a reason behind it all. Paul wrote of the days preceding the revealing of Antichrist to the world in 2 Thessalonians 2:6–8:

> And now ye know what withholdeth that he might be revealed in his time. For the mystery of iniquity doth already

work: only he who now letteth will let, until he be taken out of the way. And then shall that Wicked be revealed, whom the Lord shall consume with the spirit of his mouth, and shall destroy with the brightness of his coming.

The world must be prepared to receive the Antichrist when he comes. The influence of the Holy Spirit, working in Christians before this present world, must be removed from the scene. And as there comes a falling away within the visible church, there must at the same time come a falling away of the secular world from the bounds of decency and order established by God. The minds of men have to be reverted to the condition before the Flood; their thoughts were only evil continually. This must be done before the nations will receive and worship such an evil and wicked man as the Antichrist as their god and savior.

According to *Vine's Dictionary of Old and New Testament Words*, the "spirit of iniquity" that must be in order for the Antichrist means not everything that is unrighteous, unholy, evil, and wicked, but a contempt for everything that is holy and righteous. That is where we are today when the news media and those in authority express only contempt for the Christians who still obey the Word of God.

The spirit of iniquity, meaning everything unclean, filthy, and ungodly, is sweeping across the earth. Behind it is, according to the Bible, all the spirit and influence of a demonic personality called Antichrist.

All the scriptures in the Old Testament which speak of the coming of Antichrist project his presence upon the earth as a future event. All the prophecies in the New Testament speak of him as being a living personality, or a living spirit, who is waiting for his own time to make his appearance. Paul wrote in his day, this "mystery of iniquity" doth already work. John said of the spirit of antichrist in the year A.D. 90, "... even now already is it in the world." The word "antichrist" means the opposite of God's Messiah, the Lord Jesus Christ.

By the corrupting of the minds of men today, and the falling away from all that is of God, the world is being prepared to receive this wicked man. This corrupting spirit that is in the world today bears evidence that the Antichrist may already be present upon the earth.

Of the evil days that would come in the end of the age, we read in the little Epistle of Jude, verses 20–25:

> But ye, beloved, building up yourselves on your most holy faith, praying in the Holy Ghost, Keep yourselves in the love of God, looking for the mercy of our Lord Jesus Christ unto eternal life. And of some have compassion, making a difference: And others save with fear, pulling them out of the fire; hating even the garment spotted by the flesh. Now unto him that is able to keep you from falling, and to present you faultless before the presence of his glory with exceeding joy, To the only wise God our Saviour, be glory and majesty, dominion and power, both now and ever. Amen.

Obama's Plan to Sodomize America

One of the first official acts of Barack Obama upon becoming president of the United States was to issue a proclamation designating June, the traditional month of brides, as LGBT (or homosexual) Month. According to Obama, this was done to honor this minority segment of the U.S. population (1.7 percent) as this nation's most important citizens. The full text of the proclamation was carried in the June 27, 2009, edition of *San Francisco Pride*. The reason for dedicating a month to honor homosexuals was stated in the opening sentence:

> LGBT [Lesbian, Gay, Bisexual, Transgender] Americans have made and continue to make great and lasting contributions that continue to strengthen the fabric of American society; LGBT Americans have mobilized the nation to respond to the domestic HIV/AIDS epidemic, and played a vital role in broadening the country's response in the HIV epidemic.

This opening statement regarding the actual role homosexuals have played in U.S. history and the president's appraisal of their alerting other citizens to the need of solving the AIDS curse on humanity is beyond rational comprehension. Obama's narcissistic mindset aims to change the truth into a lie and a lie into the truth. It is a known fact that AIDS was first recognized as a new disease in 1981, when a number of young gay men in New York and Los Angeles were diagnosed with symptoms not usually seen in individuals with healthy immune systems. Originally named GRIDS for Gay Related Immune Deficiency Syndrome, AIDS is mainly transmitted through sexual activity and has already caused the deaths of hundreds of millions of people worldwide. In his book *Real Change*, Newt Gingrich shares that within three counties in Florida, AIDS victims hit Medicare for over $480 million in just six months. Evidence indicates that AIDS victims are bankrupting Medicare and robbing senior citizens of this insurance for which they have paid through salary deductions. The president continues in the next section of his homosexual proclamation:

> I am proud to be the first president to appoint LGBT candidates to Senate-confirmed positions in the first 100 days of an administration. These individuals embody the best qualities we seek in public service.

The fact is that the Senate complained that Obama was appointing "czars" without confirmation. The record also indicates that he appointed over 150 homosexuals to high government offices with administrative responsibilities. It is difficult to name anyone in the new administration who is not a homosexual and if, as Obama says, these are indeed the best people, he would seem to include himself. In 2008 a Minnesota man named Larry Sinclair came forward and claimed that in 1999 he used cocaine with the then-Illinois legislator and participated in homosexual acts with him. Sinclair charges that Obama smoked crack cocaine in the limo while Sinclair snorted powdered cocaine provided by the legislator. He says the two met in an upscale Chicago lounge before leaving in Sinclair's limousine where the drug use and sex took place for the first time. Sinclair, who says he is willing to submit to a polygraph test to validate his claims, stated, "My motivation for making this public is my desire for a presidential candidate to be honest," Sinclair told World Net Daily by telephone. "I didn't want the sex thing to come out. But I think it is important for the candidate to be honest about his drug use as late as 1999."

As to future plans for the homosexual segment of the population, the president continued:

My administration has partnered with the LGBT community to advance a wide range of initiatives. At the international level, I have joined efforts at the United Nations to decriminalize homosexuality around the world ... These measures include supporting civil unions, ... ensuring adoption rights, and ending existing "Don't Ask, Don't Tell" policies in a way that strengthens the armed forces and national security.

Mr. Obama admits, or professes, that he is not just a member of the Democratic Party, but he is also a member of the LGBT Party and that he will work to accomplish all homosexual goals while in office. These goals were set forth in the *Gay Community News* publication on February 15, 1987, in an article titled "The Gay Manifesto," written by pen name Michael Swift:

We shall sodomize your sons, emblems of your feeble masculinity, of your shallow dreams and vulgar lies. We shall seduce them in your schools, in your dormitories, in your gymnasiums, in your locker rooms, in your sports arenas, in your seminaries, in your youth groups, in your movie theater bathrooms, in your army bunkhouses, in your truck stops, in your all male clubs, in your houses of Congress, wherever men are with men together. Your sons shall become our minions and do our bidding. They will be recast in our image. They will come to crave and adore us. ... All laws banning homosexual activity will be revoked. Instead, legislation shall be passed which engenders love between men. All homosexuals must stand together as brothers; we must be united artistically, philosophically, socially, politically and financially. We will triumph only when we present a common face to the vicious heterosexual enemy. If you dare to cry faggot, fairy, queer, at us, we will stab you in your cowardly hearts and defile your dead, puny bodies. . . . There will be no compromises. We are not middle-class weaklings. Highly intelligent, we are the natural aristocrats of the human race, and steely-minded aristocrats never settle for less. Those who oppose us will be exiled. We shall raise vast private armies, as Mishima did, to defeat you. We shall conquer the world because warriors inspired by and banded together by homosexual love and honor are invincible as were the ancient Greek soldiers. The family unit—spawning ground of lies, betrayals, mediocrity, hypocrisy and violence—will be abolished. The family unit, which only dampens imagination and curbs free will, must be eliminated. . . . All churches who condemn us will be closed. Our only gods are handsome young men.

There has been much debate over the intent of "The Gay Manifesto." Some in the gay community shrug it off as a sarcastic joke, claiming it was written to mock those against the homosexual agenda. However, most in the gay community embrace it as a battle hymn for the LGBT movement. To those of us standing against the sodomizing of our nation and its values, "The Gay Manifesto" is a very real, and very terrifying, threat.

One of the goals of the Communist Party in weakening the United States was to use homosexuality as stated in Agenda 21. One specific goal was to infiltrate the armed forces. This was started by Bill Clinton during his presidency through the "Don't Ask, Don't Tell" program under which sixteen thousand homosexuals enlisted. However some twelve thousand had to be dismissed because they not only told, they did what homosexuals do.

Another of the stated goals of the homosexual conspiracy is the destruction of the family unit. God made Adam first and then Eve and the couple subsequently had two children, Cain and Abel. God established the family with one man and one woman. While this order may vary in some religions and cultures, all still maintain that the family begins with a man and a woman. Without family, no civilization, social order, or government can exist. Without this continuing relationship between the sexes, humanity degenerates to the level of animals. President Obama ordered that the Defense of Marriage Act not be defended by the federal government, and in a statement referenced by Yahoo! News on June 23, 2011, President Obama indicated he saw no difference between the marriage of a man and a woman or the marriage of two of the same sex.

Seven states have made same-sex marriages legal, the latest being New York. Catholic bishop Dimmarzio stated in a June 30, 2011, *CNS* news item that the Christian marriage has been demonized by both Democrats and Republicans, that the pillar of civilization has been destroyed, and that no senator, congressman, or government representative be allowed to enter any Catholic church in his parish.

This nation of some 300 million does not yet realize what is happening. According to the Department of Defense budget report on July 7, 2011, the spending will increase greatly due to the Defense of Marriage Act being trashed and the president's acceptance of same-sex marriages, because homosexual mates will now have the same rights to home expenses and support as Army wives.

Obama's appointment of Kevin Jennings (founder of GLSEN [Gay, Lesbian, & Straight Education Network] and one of the most outspoken homosexual activists in the world) to head the Department of Education has now led to the demand that all schoolbooks include the history and lives of so-called famous homosexuals (Fox News, July 6, 2011). *CNS* reported a homosexual party sponsored by the Department of Education. Kathleen Sebelius, another Obama appointee, stated this party was to "insure that LGBT students' rights were protected." Now, many universities in the United States are granting LGBT degrees. A federal tax grant (your money) was given to the Gay Straight Alliance Network to teach homosexual youth to perform safer sex to keep the AIDS statistics down.

Many major government departments in Washington, D.C., now have inner homosexual departments with websites. When was our Constitution amended to allow separate inner subversive units, paid for by taxpayer's dollars, whose purpose so stated is to teach our children how to "safely" sodomize each other and close our churches? The Department of Justice has a homosexual department and website headed, "DoJ PRIDE—The Official Web Presence for LGBT Employees and Their Allies." The website is composed of eight pages on the mission and purpose for the Department of Justice, but summarizes it as follows:

> Besides conducting outreach to prospective employees, DoJ Pride sponsors brown-bag lectures featuring experts in the LGBT community discussing issues of importance in DoJ members, such as marriage equality. Finally, through its yearly Pride Month Celebration and Award Ceremony, DoJ

Pride has taken an active role in recognizing the work of LGBT supporters inside the Department of Justice, the Federal Government, and the Nation.

There are sixteen references in the books of the prophets to warn nations against committing the sins of Sodom and Gomorrah. Israel's two good kings, Asa and Josiah, began their reigns by trashing the sodomites' houses, probably bathhouses, and chasing them out of town. There are six references to Sodom and Gomorrah in the Gospels, and Jesus was not exactly suggesting these cities as vacation resorts.

Paul began his letter to the Christians in Rome to warn them against becoming morally and spiritually corrupted by that homosexually-saturated society. Paul warned the Christians about homosexuals who sin against God's created order:

> For this cause God gave them up unto vile affections: for even their women did change the natural use into that which is against nature: And likewise also the men, leaving the natural use of the woman, burned in their lust one toward another; men with men working that which is unseemly, and receiving in themselves that recompence of their error which was meet. And even as they did not like to retain God in their knowledge, God gave them over to a reprobate mind, to do those things which are not convenient; ... Who knowing the judgment of God, that they which commit such things are worthy of death, not only do the same, but have pleasure in them that do them.
>
> —Romans 1:26–28, 32

When Peter wrote his last epistle, he knew that within a few days he would be crucified, and he evidently felt he had to leave the warning to Christians that they must not follow the example of Sodom and Gomorrah (2 Peter 2:6). (I did not teach from the *Southern Baptist Quarterly* lesson for July 3, 2011, because it indicated that the sin Peter referenced was gluttony or overeating.)

Jude, the half-brother of Jesus, was determined to write an epistle on the love of God in sending his brother Jesus to die for the sins of the world. However the Holy Spirit stopped him and told him to write to the churches warning about sodomites in the pulpit:

> For there are certain men crept in unawares, who were before of old ordained to this condemnation, ungodly men, turning the grace of our God into lasciviousness, and denying the only Lord God, and our Lord Jesus Christ. . . . Even as Sodom and Gomorrha, and the cities about them in like manner, giving themselves over to fornication, and going after strange flesh, are set forth for an example, suffering the vengeance of eternal fire. Likewise also these filthy dreamers defile the flesh, despise dominion, and speak evil of dignities. —Jude verses 4, 7–8

The prophet Daniel noted that the Antichrist will not desire women which indicates the Antichrist could be a homosexual, and what is happening today is at least part of the spirit of iniquity that is paving the way for universal acceptance of this man of sin.

While all the world seems to be falling into the devil's trap, there is One who is able to keep you from falling, and out of an evil and wicked world, to present you clean, and holy, and faultless to the Father in Heaven. He is the Lord Jesus Christ. Keep trusting in Him.

The Son of Perdition

As we have already brought out, there is a change in the verb tense in reference to the coming Antichrist in the Old Testament as we get into the New Testament. The Old Testament prophecies indicate the coming of the "Wicked One" to be future, whereas, in the New Testament he is presented as already being in existence.

Warnings are given in the prophecies from the Old Testament for Israel not to be foolish and accept a false prince as their messiah in the last days. For example, we note the words of the prophet in Ezekiel 21:25–27: "And thou, profane wicked prince of Israel, whose day is come, when iniquity shall have an end, Thus saith the Lord God; Remove the diadem, and take off the crown: this shall not be the same: exalt him that is low, and abase him that is high. I will overturn, overturn, overturn, it: and it shall be no more, until he come whose right it is; and I will give it him."

The identity of the Antichrist as that "Wicked One" is common in both the Old Testament and the New Testament. He is also called a prince of Israel, which indicates that he will be at least partly Jewish. He will not only be wicked, he will be profane, rejecting the "God of his fathers" (Daniel 11:37), and his speech will be filled with continual blasphemies against all that is holy and sacred (Revelation 13:6).

In speaking of the Antichrist in 2 Thessalonians 2:3, Paul calls him "that man of sin," not just "a" man of sin. This reference immediately identifies the Antichrist as a particular person. The apostle also speaks of his "revealing" as "the son of perdition," and not just "a" son of perdition. A thing or person cannot be revealed unless such an entity is already in existence—for example, the revealing or unveiling of a painting.

Jesus Christ is seated at the right hand of the Father until the time for His revealing to the world as King of Kings and Lord of Lords (Revelation 19). Likewise, the selection of definite articles used by Paul when speaking of the revealing of the "man of sin" as Antichrist signifies that the Wicked One was in existence in a state of perdition at the time Paul wrote to the church at Thessalonica. This conclusion is verified by the very definition of the word perdition, which is interpreted thus in the *Critical Lexicon and Concordance:* "Loss, destruction, ruin; the end pronounced upon all who, having heard the summons to repentance and faith in Christ, have persisted in impenitence. The loss of all that such ever had, or might have had for ever; the destruction of such, in body, soul, spirit, and utter and final ruin which will not be reversed."

It is understood that all who reject the salvation of God offered through the Lord Jesus Christ who died for sin will go into perdition—an irreversible state of eternal shame and torment. However, the Bible speaks of "the son of perdition" in the same sense it speaks of "THE Son of God." We know there are many "sons of God." Adam is called "a son of God" because he was a direct creation of God (Luke 3:38). The angels are also called "sons of God" because they, too, are direct creations of the Creator (Genesis 6:2). Christians are "sons of God" by adoption through faith in Jesus Christ (Romans 8:14–16). But, there is only one "THE only begotten Son of God." According to the same scriptural rule, there are many sons of perdition, but there is only one individual who is "THE son of perdition."

In considering clues to the possible identity of Antichrist, keep in mind that this evil and wicked person will be in the world when Christ comes the second time. When the Lord returns, He will fulfill all the promises that are associated with His glorious reign given in the Old Testament. He will heal the sick, banish war, restore nature to its edenic perfection, enforce peace and justice, and rule the nations with a rod of iron. But all the promises concerning the Messiah, Jesus Christ, were fulfilled in type at His first coming. He opened the eyes of the blind, opened the ears of the deaf, made the lame to leap as a deer, etc. All these things He did, we are informed, so that the prophecies might be fulfilled and Israel be without excuse. It is noted in Zechariah 14:4 that at that time the Lord will be King over "all the earth," He will stand upon Mount Olivet, and the mountain will split. When the time came for Jesus to present His claim to the throne of David, He departed from the Temple and went to Mount Olivet, but instead of standing, the biblical symbol for taking possession, He sat down. This gesture indicated that Jesus knew that He would be rejected; nevertheless, the promise was fulfilled in type.

The last prophecy recorded in the Old Testament is given in Malachi 4:5, "Behold, I will send you Elijah the prophet before the coming of the great and dreadful day of the LORD." When Jesus was asked the question where Elijah was, if He was indeed the Messiah, He pointed to John the Baptist, and answered that John would be Elijah if Israel would receive Him as Lord and King. And inasmuch as every prophecy concerning the appearing of the Messiah was fulfilled in part during the earthly ministry of Jesus, it is obvious that the Wicked Prince who would betray the Son of David and try to steal His throne must also have been present, at least in type, at the time. It seems apparent that the man who perfectly fits the prophetic type was Judas Iscariot.

In light of the definition of perdition, as pertaining to a state of utter ruin and damnation without end, let us think for a moment concerning the possible identity of "THE son of perdition." The greatest prophetic identifying clue to the identity of Antichrist is that he will deny that Jesus Christ has already come in the flesh, and make the vast majority of the world believe the lie. And, if we were to consider every man and woman who ever lived from Adam and Eve to this present time, who had the greatest opportunity to come to know Jesus Christ as both Lord and Savior, and yet turned away and not only rejected so great salvation, but denied Him as God's Son come in the flesh, that person would have to be Judas Iscariot. Judas, without question, would have to head the all-time list of all people who could have known without reservation that Jesus was the Christ, yet turned away and denied Him. Judas walked with Jesus for three and a half years; he witnessed the miracles of Jesus; he heard the messages of Jesus; and he heard the multitudes say, "No man ever spake like this man." Yet Judas never once considered receiving Jesus Christ as the Messiah. Jesus said of this lost disciple in John 17:12, "While I was with them in the world, I kept them in thy name: those that thou gavest me I have kept, and none of them is lost, but

THE SON OF PERDITION. . . ." It is evident that Judas was in an irreversible state of eternal damnation, even when he was numbered among the twelve.

Jesus called Judas *the son of perdition,* and Paul wrote of the Antichrist in 2 Thessalonians 2:3–4: "Let no man deceive you by any means: for that day shall not come, except there come a falling away first, and that man of sin be revealed, THE SON OF PERDITION; Who opposeth and exalteth himself above all that is called God, or that is worshipped; so that he as God sitteth in the temple of God, shewing himself that he is God."

Notice again that the definite article "the" indicates there is only one "son of perdition." Inasmuch as the title is given to one man who lived in the past in a state of perdition, and to a man to arise in the future who will be in a state of perdition when he comes, we have to consider the possibility that both men, Judas and the Antichrist, may be one and the same person.

The words of Jesus concerning Judas in John 6:70 are also of particular interest: ". . . Have not I chosen you twelve, and one of you is a devil?" The most quoted Bible authorities on the Greek text agree that the indefinite article "a" in the verse was added by the translators. What Jesus actually said of Judas was, ". . . one of you [meaning Judas] is devil. . . ." *Fausset's Bible Encyclopedia and Dictionary* says of this scripture that the Greek word for devil used by Jesus, in referring to Judas, does not "merely mean demon, the Greek word always used for the evil spirit possessing a body, but 'devil,' used only of Satan himself."

In the selecting of another to take the place of Judas, Luke wrote in Acts 1:24–25, ". . . of this ministry and apostleship, from which Judas by transgression fell, that he might go to his own place." Again, we should ponder the meaning of Judas going to "his own place," a reference applied to no other human being at death.

In the Old Testament, Israel is warned against the wicked and deceitful prince who will intercede to make a covenant for them, but after three and a half years he commits the "abomination of desolation" prophesied by Daniel. According to the Bible, this evil deed consists of stopping the daily sacrifice in the Temple, informing all the world that the biblical account of Jesus Christ and His claim to be the Messiah is a myth, and then presenting his claim to be Christ. With the aid of the False Prophet, the Antichrist will demand that all the world worship him as God or be killed. It will be at this time that the False Messiah turns against the Jews, and then they will have to flee to the wilderness and the mountains to hide. Most prophetic Bible scholars believe Israel's hiding place will be in Petra (Matthew 24:15–21; Revelation 12). The reason for Israel's flight is presented in type in Psalm 55:11–13: "Wickedness is in the midst thereof: deceit and guile depart not from her streets. For it was not an enemy that reproached me; then I could have borne it: neither was it he that hated me that did magnify himself against me; then I would have hid myself from him: But it was thou, a man mine equal, my guide, and mine acquaintance."

Dr. Arthur W. Pink, noted Bible expositor, said of this messianic psalm:

> These verses describe not only the base treachery of Judas toward Christ, but they also announce how he shall yet,

when reincarnated in the Antichrist, betray and desert Israel. The relation of Antichrist to Israel will be precisely the same as that of Judas to Christ. He will pose as the friend of the Jews, but later he will come out in his true character. In the tribulation period, the nation shall taste the bitterness of betrayal and desertion by one who masqueraded as a "familiar friend." Hence, we have here the first hint that the Antichrist will be Judas reincarnated.

More knowledge was given to the Apostle John by the Holy Spirit about the person and reign of Antichrist than any other writer of Holy Scripture. Only John described this agent of Satan as antichrist, the total negative of the Lord Jesus Christ. By reading in sequence the Gospel of John, the First Epistle of John, and the Revelation of John, we have a composite picture of the beginning and the end of the "son of perdition."

There have been some very credible theologians who have understood from a careful study of scriptures referencing the Antichrist that he will be a reincarnation of a former evil enemy of Jesus Christ. Such suggestions have included King Herod, Emperor Nero, and others. However, the most obvious candidate has been Judas. We cannot say definitely that the Antichrist will be a reincarnated evil person of the past, but if such would be the case, then we would think Judas would be the one.

Judas was the only one of the twelve disciples who was not a Galilean, and little is known about his family or background. There is not a good word said about him in the entire Bible. Psalm 109 provides a remarkably prophetic view of the relationship of Judas to Jesus Christ. Verses 6 through 11 speak of Judas thusly: "Set thou a wicked man over him: and let Satan stand at his right hand. When he shall be judged, let him be condemned: and let his prayer become sin. Let his days be few; and let another take his office. . . . Let the extortioner catch all that he hath; and let the strangers spoil his labour."

This part of the messianic Psalm 109 refers to the betrayal of Jesus by Judas, his evil nature, the buying of a potter's field with the bribe money, and the appointment of Matthias to take the place of the fallen disciple. Verses 13 through 15 of the same psalm relate to the judgment Judas brought upon himself for his terrible sin: "Let his posterity be cut off; and in the generation following let their name be blotted out. Let the iniquity of his fathers be remembered with the LORD; and let not the sin of his mother be blotted out. Let them be before the LORD continually, that he may cut off the memory of them from the earth."

Judas was the tool of the religious element of the generation in Israel at the time Jesus Christ offered them the Kingdom. In the Temple Discourse (Matthew 23), Jesus pronounced judgment on that generation. Jesus was born in 4 B.C., so the Temple Discourse was delivered in A.D. 30. Forty is the Jewish number of testing. The generation of Israel who refused to believe God and cross the Jordan wandered in the wilderness for forty years, and they were cut off. At the end of forty years, after Jesus pronounced judgment upon the generation who refused to believe that He was the Messiah, that generation was also cut off. But Jesus spoke of a second generation in the Olivet Discourse. He said of the signs given in Matthew 24 concerning His Second Coming, ". . . This generation shall not pass, till all these things be fulfilled"(vs. 34). In the Temple Discourse, Jesus warned of another judgment that would come on a second generation, the generation of Israel in the days of His return. The second generation of Israelites spoken about in the Olivet Discourse will see the refounding of Israel as a nation. They will be the ones who will receive the false messiah who will come in his own name (John 5:43). Two-thirds of the second generation will be cut off from the Kingdom (Zechariah 13:8–9). The remaining one-third of the last generation will say, ". . . Blessed is he that cometh in the name of the Lord" (Matthew 23:39).

The prophecies concerning Judas in Psalm 109 relating to his treachery are divided into two different generations. God keeps time by the Jew, but when the Jew is out of the land, time stops. Thus, the first twelve verses relate to Judas in his betrayal of Jesus at the first advent of Christ. The remainder of the psalm concerning the judgment of Judas when he will be completely and forever cut off, and his name remembered no more, is connected with the second advent of the Lord. The things which are to happen to Judas in the second generation seem to parallel the final end of Antichrist.

There are some who believe that the Antichrist will be a great world personality who will be killed and brought back to life, and possessed by the devil. However, there are sound scriptural reasons for believing that the Antichrist will be an evil man who has lived in the past, and Satan is keeping him in perdition, waiting for world conditions to develop favorably where he can be brought forth. The Scriptures indicate this is to be the case, and Judas Iscariot, "THE son of perdition" is the most likely candidate.

However, regardless of the personal identity of Antichrist,

we know that his spirit, the spirit of iniquity, is sweeping the world today to prepare the way for this "man of sin." When the iniquity of this present age is brought to a peak, then the Antichrist will be revealed. We must consider the possibility that this Wicked One may be in the world today. This being true, then the individual should be making preparations lest that day come upon him as a thief in the night. The Word of God declares in 1 Thessalonians 4:13–18 that if you will believe that Jesus Christ, the Son of God, died for your sins; that He arose from the grave to become the firstfruits of resurrection; and you receive Him as your Savior and Lord, you will be saved from the coming "day of wrath," and inherit eternal life.

Influence of Antichrist on Today's Ecology

Jesus Christ said of general social conditions that would prevail in the last days, "But as the days of Noe were, so shall also the coming of the Son of man be" (Matthew 24:37). And how were the days of Noah? The answer is provided in Genesis 6:5, 12–13: "And God saw that the wickedness of man was great in the earth, and that every imagination of the thoughts of his heart was only evil continually. . . . And God looked upon the earth, and, behold, it was corrupt; for all flesh had corrupted his way upon the earth. . . . For the earth is filled with violence . . ." (Genesis 6:5, 12–13).

The Bible informs us in many places about the angels that sinned, and the consequences of their sins—upheavals and chaos in the heavens. Astronomers have concluded that a great catastrophe visited our own solar system about ten thousand years ago. It is noted in Hebrews 1:10 that the heavens came into being by the work of God's hands, and all things in the beginning were created good and clean by the Creator. But the heavens were made unclean by the sin of the angels who followed Satan in the rebellion. Ezekiel 28:18 indicates that Satan has defiled his sanctuaries in the heavens through his own iniquity.

Likewise, creation on earth that was good in the beginning has been defiled by the sin of mankind. When sin entered the caretakers of the creation on earth, God spoke in Genesis 3:17–18: "... cursed is the ground for thy sake; in sorrow shalt thou eat of it all the days of thy life; Thorns also and thistles shall it bring forth to thee..." (Genesis 3:17–18). But the sin in mankind grew and multiplied, and all the earth became filled with iniquity and violence, and God cleansed His creation on this planet with a flood.

Nevertheless, the corruption of the world by sin before the Flood left its scars on nature. God spoke again in Genesis 8:21–22; 9:2:

> ... the imagination of man's heart is evil from his youth; neither will I again smite any more every thing living, as I have done. While the earth remaineth, seedtime and harvest, and cold and heat, and summer and winter, and day and night shall not cease.... And the fear of you and the dread of you shall be upon every beast of the earth, and upon every fowl of the air, upon all that moveth upon the earth, and upon all the fishes of the sea....

Hot days, blizzards, droughts, famines, the bite of a snake, the startled jump of a deer before the hunter, and the angry bark of the watchdog are all manifestations of the effect of sin in the human heart upon nature. This truth is openly declared in Romans 8:19–22:

> For the earnest expectation of the creature waiteth for the manifestation of the sons of God. For the creature was made subject to vanity, not willingly, but by reason of him who hath subjected the same in hope, Because the creature itself also shall be delivered from the bondage of corruption into the glorious liberty of the children of God. For we know that the whole creation groaneth and travaileth in pain together until now.

The trees, the flowers, the grass, the beasts of the field and the forests are all affected by the sin of mankind. All creation on earth is waiting for Jesus Christ to come and suppress the sin of man so that the deserts will again blossom like the rose, and the lambs lie down with the lions. But we are instructed that, in the last days, sin will not be suppressed; it will be unleashed. As previously noted, iniquity in the end time will greatly increase (2 Thessalonians 2:7). It is also prophesied of the increase of sin and iniquity in the last days in 2 Timothy 3:1–4, 13:

> This know also, that in the last days perilous times shall come. For men shall be lovers of their own selves, covetous, boasters, proud, blasphemers, disobedient to parents, unthankful, unholy, Without natural affection, trucebreakers, false accusers, incontinent, fierce, despisers of those that are good, Traitors, heady, highminded, lovers of pleasures more than lovers of God . . . evil men and seducers shall wax worse and worse, deceiving, and being deceived.

As we have adequately proven from Scripture, there is a relation between the sinfulness of mankind and the ecology of earth. There is a direct relationship between the environmental problems and the exceeding sinfulness of sin that emanates from society in general. There is a direct relationship between the rising crime rate, and air pollution, weather conditions, the energy crisis, and the endangered species of wildlife. Nature reacts when men rebel en masse against the Creator. The plain statement of Revelation 6:8 is that the beasts of the earth will rise up against men when the nations join together in iniquity to worship the "man of sin."

God gives many warnings when judgment us about to fall, and when men fail to heed God's Word, or the signs of the times, the Lord speaks to them through the medium to which they are listening at the time. For example, God spoke to Balaam through his ass when the prophet failed to listen to the voice of God. Balaam's ass today is the movies and/or television, because that is the medium to which most people are attuned.

Some time ago, a movie called *The Birds* was produced, and this movie has subsequently been shown a number of times on television. In this movie, for no apparent reason, the birds began gathering in droves and attacking people in such numbers and with such ferocity that men, women, and children were killed and mutilated. It was a terrifying sight to see flocks of birds pecking out people's eyes and puncturing their blood veins. Whether the producers of the movie were Bible students or not is not known, but the film itself had a Tribulation setting. Even the birds will attack people in great numbers in the day when the "man of sin" rules as dictator of this world. We read in Revelation 19:17–18, 21, of this unusual ecological upheaval:

And I saw an angel standing in the sun; and he cried with a loud voice, saying to all the fowls that fly in the midst of heaven, Come and gather yourselves together unto the supper of the great God; That ye may eat the flesh of kings, and the flesh of captains, and the flesh of mighty men, and the flesh of horses, and of them that sit on them, and the flesh of all men, both free and bond, both small and great.... And all the fowls were filled with their flesh.

In another movie titled *The Frogs,* insects and animals rose up in unison and attacked populations on every continent—either chewing masses of people to pieces or stinging them to death. Jesus said that in the last days there would be earthquakes in diverse places, and in Revelation it is reported that during the Tribulation period, earthquakes will be so severe that mountains will be leveled and islands will sink into the oceans. A recent movie called *Earthquake* depicted the terror that would grip the world when these terrible events come.

Although the yearly number of earthquakes have increased from an average of eight thousand in 1986 to thirty-two thousand in 2011, and wars and rumors of wars continue as well as pandemic diseases like AIDS, the basic stability of environmental conditions have remained static, as God promised:

And the LORD smelled a sweet savour; and the LORD said in his heart, I will not again curse the ground any more for man's sake; for the imagination of man's heart is evil from his youth; neither will I again smite any more every thing living, as I have done. While the earth remaineth, seedtime and harvest, and cold and heat, and summer and winter, and day and night shall not cease. —Genesis 8:21-22

However, with the advent of the United Nations programs to form a world consensus on political and economic issues, the Club of Rome and other like-minded universalists looked for a common enemy the nations could unite against, since it was difficult to unite under a common cause. The common enemy of mankind, proposed by men like Maurice Strong, a billionaire and director of the United Nations Environment Programme, was CO_2. CO_2 is a harmless gas composed of two parts oxygen and one part carbon. It is also called "greenhouse gas" because greenhouse farmers pump CO_2 into their greenhouses to produce more vegetables and fruit. Animals breathe in oxygen and emit CO_2, and plants absorb CO_2 and give off oxygen. Approximately ninety-seven percent of CO_2 in the air comes from the oceans, a very small amount of the remaining three percent comes from decay or animal activity, such as breathing, or from fires or engine exhaust. To make CO_2 a common enemy rather than a blessing of nature, temperature gauges were placed in locations where there was more sunlight or heat to make it appear that earth's temperature was increasing. The propaganda line went out that the ice caps would melt and flood cities in coastal areas, and the poor polar bears were starving because the ice was melting and they could not get out to eat the seals. Latest reports indicate polar bear populations have actually greatly increased and that there is no global warming.

The first United Nations Earth Summit was held in June 1992 in Rio de Janeiro, with twenty-four hundred government representatives from 172 nations and an additional fifteen thousand from other international organizations. In December 1997 another U.N.- sponsored environmental conference was held in Kyoto, Japan, which again proposed an international environment disaster was imminent resulting from CO_2 emissions. Reduction percentages were established for every single nation. At the writing of this book, 191 nations have ratified the Kyoto Protocol. The four that failed to accept the Kyoto CO_2 reduction are Afghanistan, Andorra, South Sudan, and the United States. It is obvious that the only nation of any consequence that has not ratified and accepted this obvious lie is the United States. Even so, due to the propaganda disseminated by the news media on this issue, it is probable that the majority in our own country today believe that CO_2 is a cause for so-called global warming.

Greenland is called Greenland because at one time, over a thousand years ago, it was green because the earth was warmer. At the present time, we are coming out from the Little Ice Age because the nuclear fusion action of the sun has increased. Below is a chart showing the meandering average temperature line over the past two thousand years.

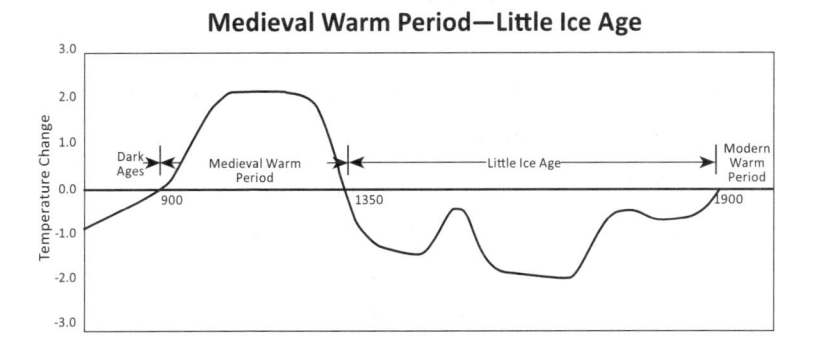

Medieval Warm Period—Little Ice Age

Dr. Blick's appraisal of the claims of some global warming advocates is as follows:

Man-Made Global Warming
Is History's Greatest Delusion

The warming of Earth during the twentieth century was due to large increases in sunspots and solar irradiance. During this time period astronomers observed the sun warming Jupiter, Mars, Saturn, Neptune, and Pluto. The evidence: the shrinking of CO_2 ice caps; moons changing from solid ice to liquid; frozen nitrogen turning to gas etc. Man's activity on Earth did not warm the planets. During this time period, CO_2 bubbled out of our warming ocean (just as it bubbles out of a warming glass of carbonated beverage) and increased the amount of atmospheric CO_2. The active sun caused both an increase in temperature of 0.6° F, and an increase in atmospheric CO_2. Man has only caused a 3 percent increase in atmospheric CO_2, due to his use of fossil fuels. Scientists have computed the global warming in the twentieth century, due to burning fossil fuel, to be a miniscule 0.01-0.09° F. This is too small to measure since it is much less than the natural temperature fluctuations due to the variation in clouds and water vapor. Expect any temperature increase in the next 100 years due to man's activity also to be too small to detect.

Temperature data available since the late 1800s have shown the following years for the record high temperatures for each continent: Europe—1881; Australia—1889; South America—1905; Oceania—1912; North America—1913;

Africa—1922; Asia—1942; Antarctica—1974. If man's burning of fossil fuels caused global warming, one would expect that most record-high temperatures would have occurred in the last few decades. But they did not.

The distribution of all-time high temperature records of our fifty states also fails to show any evidence for man-made global warming. Twenty-four of the fifty states had their record high temperature in the 1930s. Thirty-three (two-thirds) of the states had their record high temperatures during the period of 1880s–1930s. During this time period, far less CO_2 was emitted into the atmosphere by the burning of fossil fuels than in the last sixty years. Since 2002, we've had a ten-year period of global cooling due to a less active sun (fewer sunspots). The falling temperatures occurred in spite of increasing CO_2, which directly contradicts the Gore/U.N. man-made global warming theory.

Hurricanes and other tropical cyclones are at their lowest activity for thirty years. Sea level has risen at one foot/century, and has not risen at all for the past three years. The polar bear population is up fivefold since the 1940s. Antarctic Ocean ice has been growing for thirty years. Greenland's average ice-sheet thickness grew by 2 inches/year from 1993–2003.

Man-made global warming is not science . . . it is a political tool to try to abolish the use of fossil fuels. He who controls carbon (fossil fuels) controls the people!

The Apostle Paul advised those living in the last days that the Antichrist would come to power because the world would believe a lie.

And then shall that Wicked be revealed, whom the Lord shall consume with the spirit of his mouth, and shall destroy with the brightness of his coming: Even him, whose coming is after the working of Satan with all power and signs and lying wonders, And with all deceivableness of unrighteousness in them that perish; because they received not the love of the truth, that they might be saved. And for this cause God shall send them strong delusion, that they should believe a lie.

—2 Thessalonians 2:8–11

Before the Flood the human race had been corrupted genetically by the fallen angels that the devil had sent into the world. Only Noah was perfect, or uncorrupted. The animal world also had been changed in its order as God established, and only the pure animals were taken into the ark. Likewise, today we live in a hybrid world. God divided the nations, but today the populations are racially mixed; we have hybrid animals and hybrid plants. The January 17, 2011, edition of *Time* magazine announced that people would live to be one thousand years old, as they did before the Flood. The same article proposed that the "human era" would soon close and the best qualities in animals would be genetically mixed with human genes. Even the Department of Defense has begun programs for human enhancement.

According to Genesis 6, the world economy, including the entire world population with the exception of eight souls, was corrupted by an invasion from outer space, identified in the Bible as fallen angels. Inasmuch as God said that as it was in the days of Noah, so it would be when Jesus Christ came the second time, could this be happening again today?

On September 25, 2010, before the National Press Club, five Air Force officers testified that UFOs had invaded U.S. missile sites and suddenly disarmed intercontinental nuclear missiles. They also added in their testimony that the intelligence and power of these UFOs are beyond comprehensions. UFOs have to be one of two things—an advanced civilization from another galaxy or a second invasion of Satan's angels from his domain. Satan rules one-third of the angelic host.

In recent years the false theory of global warming has been introduced as the cause of environmental corruption, but the latest news items before me charge that global warming is a scientific fraud. But we can be sure that this corrupted earth will be burned up (2 Peter 3:10).

Josephus wrote that the sons of Seth built two great structures—one of brick and one of stone. The building of brick was destroyed in the Flood, but the building of stone—the Great Pyramid of Egypt—remains to warn the populations of earth that one day the earth will be destroyed by fire.

This is why God's people are encouraged to look for New Heavens and a New Earth wherein will dwell righteousness. How do we do that? By receiving Jesus Christ as our Lord and Savior.

Influence of Antichrist on Today's Economy

In this fifth division of the study on the general topic *Is the Antichrist Alive Today?*, we will discuss the influence of antichrist that is felt upon the economy of our day. The Apostle John said the influence, or spirit, of antichrist was manifest to some extent upon the world in his day (1 John 4:3). The Apostle Paul prophesied that the "mystery of iniquity," or the influence of antichrist, would be especially heavy upon the earth in the days preceding the revealing of this "man of sin." In no other area of the activity of mankind is the presence of antichrist so prevalent today than in the general world economy, and there is a definite reason for this to be true. Consider the following scriptures which refer to the reign of Antichrist:

1. "... in his estate shall he honour the God of forces: and a god whom his fathers knew not shall he honour with gold, and silver, and with precious stones, and pleasant things" (Daniel 11:38).
2. "He shall stretch forth his hand also upon the countries: ... he shall have power over the treasures of gold and of silver, and over all the precious things of Egypt: and the

Libyans and the Ethiopians shall be at his steps" (Daniel 11:42–43).
3. "And when he had opened the third seal, I heard the third beast say, Come and see. And I beheld, and lo a black horse; and he that sat on him had a pair of balances in his hand. And I heard a voice in the midst of the four beasts say, A measure of wheat for a penny, and three measures of barley for a penny; and see thou hurt not the oil and the wine" (Revelation 6:5–6).
4. ". . . and power was given him over all kindreds, and tongues, and nations" (Revelation 13:7).
5. "And he causeth all, both small and great, rich and poor, free and bond, to receive a mark in their right hand, or in their foreheads: And that no man might buy or sell, save he that had the mark, or the name of the beast, or the number of his name" (Revelation 13:16–17).
6. "And the merchants of the earth shall weep and mourn . . . for no man buyeth their merchandise any more" (Revelation 18:11).
7. ". . . ye rich men, weep and howl for your miseries that shall come upon you. . . . Your gold and silver is cankered. . . . Ye have heaped treasure together for the last days. . . . [T]he coming of the Lord draweth nigh" (James 5:1, 3, 8).

The general picture of the world of business as God's time for this present age gradually winds down to the midnight hour is as follows: Inflation will become so rampant that a one-pound loaf of bread will cost fifty dollars, according to the present wage scale. Oil and wine are representative of medical care in the Bible (Luke 10:34). Inflation and food shortages will increase, and the demand for medical services will increase accordingly. A man may starve to death, but he is going to have good medical attention up to the minute he draws his last breath. The Antichrist will institute a worldwide health plan. Gold and silver will be taken out of circulation, ending up in the hands of the very rich. All business, including the distribution of food, will come under the direct control of world government headed by the Antichrist. All monies will be worthless, because there will be a new exchange system—the number or mark issued by the government of a world dictator, and without this number and/or mark, a person will not be able to buy even a stick of chewing gum. Every person will be marked with a number, and every item of merchandise will be coded with a mark and a number. No person will be able to check into a hospital, be treated by a doctor, or even get a prescription filled, without a number assigned by the world governmental system.

For centuries, theologians have wondered how such a worldwide economic system could be instituted. Think of the communications network, and the complicated bookkeeping system that would be required in order to keep track of the daily business transactions of seven billion people in over two hundred nations around the globe. Before the age of the communications satellite and the computer, such a thing would have been impossible.

In 1966, we began to notice the embryo of a world economic system that was promoted by the International Monetary Fund and the World Bank. By 1969, the new money system had taken shape to the point where we made the following observation:

The new money will be simple, efficient, and force people to live within their means. It will help to handle the banking and business of the exploding millions much easier and quicker. Instead of paying employees in money or writing them a check, the employer will electronically credit, by means of a special telephone, the worker's account in the local computer bank. When the individual goes to the local supermarket, he shows his account number to the cashier at the check-out stand. His account is immediately charged, but if he is overdrawn, a red light will come on. . . . As the purchases passes the cashier, he will hold his hand open, palm outward, or a number will be on his forehead. These two places on a person's body will be the most logical place for the account number to be tattooed with a new painless tattoo gun machine. No money will change hands—no billfolds or purses will open—no delay. Everyone employed, everyone offering public service, every manufacturer, and every farmer will be required to have an account number.

Now then, let us advance from 1969 and see how our projection of the new money system has developed:

Buying With a Number

The first experience of any great consequence relating to the new economic system took place in the United States in 1971 in Upper Arlington, Ohio. We quote from the December 26, 1971, edition of *Parade* magazine:

> Can you imagine an all-day shopping trip . . . without carrying cash or even your checkbook? That's what they're

doing in this central Ohio city where 31 merchants, more than 2,000 customers, and a bank are joined in a pioneering experiment that's aimed at moving toward a cashless, checkless society.... They've dropped in to inspect the experiment from all 50 states and from Japan, Canada, Switzerland, and West Germany.... When the test period runs out in April, the project will be continued and extended....

The news report of the experiment explained how all business transactions in that city were done through computer identification of the buyer and the seller through electronic numbers. This report projected that the day would come when everyone would have to have a computer account number in order to buy or sell.

Working By a Number

How the new cashless system would relate to workers was partially explained in a United Press release dated August 31, 1971:

There has been a lot of talk about a moneyless and even a checkless society. We've seen credit cards bring about somewhat of a moneyless society. But few believe a checkless society would come about. It [already] has in several areas. The 1,300 employees of the Sarasota Florida Memorial Hospital haven't received a paycheck since January 1967.... The system is great to a Honeywell 1259 computer....

This news report projected that the day would come when no man or woman would receive a paycheck.

Banking With a Number

How the new money system ties into the banking system was explained in an article that appeared in the September 4, 1972, edition of *U.S. News & World Report,* under the heading "Checkless Society Moves Step Closer":

> California banks, which introduced the popular bank-credit-card systems ... are now preparing to take another bold step into the checkless society foretold for the future. Beginning October 16, many banks in the state will permit individual customers in California to authorize employers to deposit their pay into their checking accounts automatically. . . . If the plan proves popular with bankers and their customers in California, it is expected to become nationwide.

Your Number at the Federal Reserve

It is obvious that such a system of doing business with numbers and computers would eventually have to come under federal control. A New York Times Service news story that was carried in the January 2, 1973, edition of the *Daily Oklahoman* reported:

> The Federal Reserve System has endorsed the development of a vast nationwide network of computers to transfer money from one person to another. . . . An electronic communications network would be employed to transfer funds instantaneously ... from the account of a person making a purchase at a department store, or from the account of a company issuing a payroll check or to the account of a utility making a regular monthly billing. At the ultimate, the Federal

Reserve indicated, every home could in effect be a branch bank in the age of electronic money through the installation of a computer terminal that would be interconnected with a national money-transfer network.... Through the use of a card or similar identifying device ... this procedure will be accomplished through automated teller units conveniently located in shopping centers, and in other places handling numerous consumer sales and in the homes.

Your Banking Number Becomes an International Affair

The January 1975 issue of *Burroughs Clearing House,* a publication of the Burroughs Corporation, carried the followed news story:

> Work begins on a private international telecommunications network that will speed the movement of funds throughout Europe and also link with banks in the U.S. and Canada. Burroughs Corp. has been selected by the Society for Worldwide Interbank Financial Telecommunications to supply data processing and data communications equipment which will be used in a **new international telecommunications network** which is based in Brussels, which currently has a membership of 246 banks.

The Common Market, now the European Union, headquartered in Brussels, has denied there is a huge computer in Brussels called "The Beast," but what cannot be denied is that the capital city of the European Union is a very important link in the new international computer banking chain. The computer data, containing the individual's computer number, fed into the national system will doubtless be integrated into the international computer network, thus the American's number will become a part of the new financial order of the world.

Special Drawing Rights

Of course, when the new money system becomes a completed entity, a new monetary unit will have to be adopted. Without a doubt, the new money will be called Special Drawing Rights. The September 20, 1973, edition of *Senior Scholastics*, a secular news magazine for high school and college students, depicted on the cover a drawing of men and women as they would appear in the new economic order. They all appeared with numbers on their foreheads. The cover of the magazine was related to an article inside, which read in part:

> All buying and selling in the program will be done by computer. No currency, no change, no checks. In the program, people would receive a number that had been assigned them tattooed in their wrist or forehead. The number is put on by a laser beam and cannot be felt. The number in the body is not seen with the naked eye and is as permanent as your fingerprint. All items of consumer goods will be marked with a computer mark. The computer outlet in the store which picks up the number on the items at the checkstand will also pick up the number in the person's body and automatically total the price and deduct the amount from the person's "Special Drawing Rights" account....

Special Drawing Rights is nothing more than a computer unit. The name "Special Drawing Rights" indicates that doing business in the future will be a right granted by government. The computer SDR balance can be wiped out with a flick of the wrist by someone in Washington, Brussels, or even Jerusalem. The article in the *Senior Scholastics* predicted four things that would happen to bring in a world financial order.

1. **All computer goods will have a computer mark.** This began to take place in 1974. Today, practically every item for sale has the computer mark, even a package of chewing gum.
2. **All buying and selling will be done by computer.** This is taking place right now in city after city. The February 3, 1976, edition of our local newspaper, the *Oklahoma City Times,* carried a full-page article on page 8 entitled "Electronic Pricing Foes Speak Out." This article concerned the installation of computer checkout stands in stores throughout the state of Oklahoma. This is just an example of what has happened worldwide.
3. **All money and checks will be done away with in favor of SDR.** Quoting from the September 4, 1975, edition of the *Houston Chronicle:* "The Organization of Petroleum Exporting Countries is considering adoption of SDR pricing system for oil.... Worldwide airline passenger fares, cargo rates, and other transport transactions are all to be quoted in SDR.... The SDR is a computerized unit...." This article continued to tell of other areas in international trade and commerce where SDRs would be adopted.
4. **All citizens must have a laser tattoo number on their wrist or their forehead.** This number will be the individual's computer account number that will be picked up by

the computer checkout unit. Inasmuch as the three other parts of the plan for a new world economic order have either come to pass, or they are in the process of coming to pass, there is no reason not to assume that the fourth part of the plan will come to pass also. The November 6, 1975, edition of the *Oklahoma City Times* carried the following amazing news item: "Laser Brands Near." ". . . A university professor believes a 'laser iron' may be in [the] future. The laser beam branding iron marks steers and horses—and swimming salmon. It is quick and painless. . . . The laser destroys skin pigment. In thirty-billionths of a second a technician can stitch a brand . . . or just initials. . . ." It is certain that in a cashless society where the individual's computer number can be the difference between life and death, almost all will want their number tattooed on their forehead or in their hand. According to the Bible, this will be a requirement.

We read again of the coming economic system of Antichrist in Revelation 13:16–17: "And he causeth all, both small and great, rich and poor, free and bond, to receive a mark in their right hand, or in their foreheads: And that no man might buy or sell, save he that had the mark, or the name of the beast, or the number of his name." The next verse indicates the code prefix will be the number 666, and we will discuss the particulars of this number in a subsequent chapter.

The October 25, 1982, edition of the *Times Union,* Rochester, New York, observed: "The government is toying with the idea of giving us all numbers. If the legislation passes, we'll all have to carry national identity cards. Maybe one day we'll have the Universal Product Code imprinted on our palms... so they can run us through the scanner hooked up to a computer."

Computer and business magazines are replete with notices that the age of a new business concept is dawning—all buying and selling done with a visual telephone-computer unit. Large department stores may become extinct. A communications unit developed for the emerging market concept has been produced by the NEC Corporation, Tokyo, Japan. It is sold in the United States through National Marketing, Inc., Little Rock, Arkansas. The new technology is called "Cellular Systems." We reproduced in our monthly "Pastor's Letter" for July 1984 a picture of the device and a portion of the wording of an accompanying description given by the manufacturer, which states in part: "Available right now, the mobile phone of the future. It's from NEC. And while ten years went into its perfection, it does its job in an instant. Because with 666 possible channels, it never makes your customers wait... they simply dial and talk."

What we see developing before our eyes gives every indication of a manifestation of the influence of antichrist on today's economy. This is just another sign that the Antichrist may be in the world today.

And Now...

The preceding chronological economic order being prepared for the antichrist system was collected and presented by me between the years of 1975 and 1987. Perhaps evidence of where all this will end was reported in a CBS News item dated November 1, 2011, under the headline: "Man Fired for Not Wearing '666' Sticker."

It seems this factory worker in Georgia was simply trying to obey God's warning that he was not to take the number "666," and he was subsequently fired. While this may be an isolated incident today, it is warning about the future. According to Revelation 13, if this employee was under the antichrist system—which may be just a few years from now—he would not only be fired, he would have been beheaded.

Evidence as to whether the "beast" of Revelation 13 will be a human being or a machine is still inconclusive, as indicated in an Associated Press news item titled "IBM says it's developed chips that behave like human brain," dated August 18, 2011:

> The challenge in training a computer to behave like a human brain is technological and physiological, testing the limits of computer and brain science. But researchers from IBM Corp. say they've made a key step toward combining the two worlds.
>
> The company announced Thursday that it has built two prototype chips that it says process data more like humans digest information than the chips that now power PCs and supercomputers.

As I conclude this chapter, rabbis in Israel have concluded from their study in the Old Testament, it is time for Messiah to come. Even though they do not accept Jesus Christ at His first coming as Messiah, this is a warning that it is time for Jesus Christ to return. At the same time, the leaders of Islam have concluded that these are the last days and it is time for their Mahdi to come and kill everyone who is not a Muslim.

All the above means that it is also time for the Antichrist to make an appearance, and all who will not take his mark and number will be killed. Taking the mark and number of Antichrist will mean eternal damnation in Hell. If the reader of this book is not a Christian, then there is a probability he or she may have to make the decision to take the mark of the beast or suffer beheading.

Accept Jesus Christ as your Savior today and you will be included in those who won't ever have to make this choice:

> For the Lord himself shall descend from heaven with a shout, with the voice of the archangel, and with the trump of God: and the dead in Christ shall rise first: Then we which are alive and remain shall be caught up together with them in the clouds, to meet the Lord in the air: and so shall we ever be with the Lord. —1 Thessalonians 4:16-17

Chapter 6

Economic Agents of Antichrist

God that made the world and all things therein, seeing that he is Lord of heaven and earth, dwelleth not in temples made with hands; Neither is worshipped with men's hands, as though he needed any thing, seeing he giveth to all life, and breath, and all things; And hath made of one blood all nations of men for to dwell on all the face of the earth, and hath determined the times before appointed, and the bounds of their habitation. —Acts 17:24–26

We also read in Scripture that God divided the nations according to the number of Israel, meaning that Israel was to be a blessing, example, and leader of all nations. God divided the nations by oceans, rivers, mountains, deserts, distance, language, race, and color. After Babel, God did not want a world government ruled by godless tyrants like Nimrod. But it is the plan of Satan to reverse God's plan and bring all nations back together again under a world government ruled by his man, the Antichrist. As indicated in the previous chapter, the quickest and surest way to bring about a one-world government is economics.

I was at the Moen church in Shanghai immediately after the death of Mao and the trial of the Gang of Four in 1978. Mao was a communist dictator. I was in Russia in 1989 immediately after the fall of the Iron Curtain. Stalin was a communist dictator. I was in Cuba in 2005. Castro is a communist dictator. I have also been to Mongolia and other communist or former communist nations. The story in all concerning how they fell to communism—an atheistic political form of government—is the same. If the government takes control of all properties and financial exchange accounts or monies, then everyone is poor and must look to the central government for money. Money or food supplied by the government means control over every citizen. And so we read that the Antichrist will have control over all money and no one will eat unless they have his mark, which can be taken away in an instant. So what we have in the government of Antichrist is a world economic system.

I served in World War II in the South Pacific directing field artillery for the First Cavalry Armored Division. After WWII, the United Nations Organization was formed by internationalists who envisioned a world, as they reportedly thought, where there would be no war, no hunger, and everyone would live in peace and plenty. The United Nations' social engineers, in re-making the world to their image, concluded that poor nations were poor because the richer nations had somehow robbed them of their wealth, the United States being the most guilty. Huge loans were made to the so-called underdeveloped nations. Import taxes and embargoes were gradually removed. International billionaires like Soros took advantage of the new economic rules and moved factories from the United States to nations where labor was cheap, and then shipped the goods back at many times the cost.

When I first went to China, a motor vehicle was a rarity. Recently, the largest traffic jam in the world was reported between Beijing and Shanghai. China now has 130-story hotels the like of which we don't have here, eight- and ten-lane highways, new airports, new airplanes, etc.

Three ships, one-quarter of a mile long, ten stories high, loaded with sixteen thousand cargo containers each, sail loaded from China to Los Angeles, San Francisco, or San Diego. They unload in six hours and then head back to China for another load. The tragic thing is that even the ships are not made in the United States. They are made in Denmark. Household items, clothing, vegetables, meats, automobiles, etc., pour in from almost every nation in the world. Practically everything Americans drive, wear, eat, or sit on is made overseas. Unemployment increases as the stronger nations get weaker and the weaker nations get stronger. Walmart, the nation's largest market outlet, imports ninety-one percent of their merchandise from China.

Communism, Nazism, and socialism all come to the same eventual conclusion, which is the subversion of all classes to a single authority with no self-governing rights. The accountability of all three classes ends in a single or central dictatorship. In order to bring about a single class that is subservient to a single authority, as Bastiat brought out so plainly in his book *The Law*, the government must by legal plunder take from the rich and give to the poor.

In 1937–38, I worked for the FDR farm program telling farmers how much they could or could not plant, or how much they had to plow under in the event they planted too much. Many at that time had lost their homes during the Great Depression, so as the economy improved and Europe prepared for war, the socialistic-inclined bureaucracy thought it would be a popular government-sponsored thing to help the homeless find homes. The program called Fannie Mae was created in 1938. In 1966 Lyndon Johnson within his so-called Great Society pro-socialistic program expanded Fannie Mae again, and in 1970 he added a new sub-housing program and named it Freddie Mac. The Freddie Mac program enticed foreign investors from London, Paris, Moscow, Beijing, and to the ends of the earth, who wanted to profit on some of the nineteen percent interest rates. Both programs were expanded by Jimmy Carter, and in 1999 President Clinton practically removed all restraints. Using Acorn and its lawyer, Barack Obama, banks were literally forced to use deposits, savings, stocks, and pension funds to underwrite mortgages for practically anyone who wandered in off the street. If banks refused a mortgage, they were immediately challenged and picketed by goons without recourse. According to one report, mortgages were even granted to five million illegal residents. Any further restraints to granting mortgages were removed by the federal government which guaranteed the mortgages.

In 1999 every spare dollar possible was invested in building homes for the rich, the middle class, and the poor, including millions without income even below the poverty line. The latter category was segregated into sub-prime mortgages and sold to major financial institutions at discounts. Trillions in savings, pension funds, and deposits were invested in building millions of houses. Everyone is working, business is booming.

President Clinton, when asked about his policies, remarked, "It's for the economy, stupid!" However, even the liberal *New York Times* in its September 30, 1999, edition warned that granting all these sub-prime mortgages to low-income holders, or no-income holders, could portend a severe economic collapse. This came in the fall of 2008. There were no reserve funds to fall back on, as practically all banking reserves and pension funds had been invested in mortgages that could no longer be paid. Financial institutions like Lehman Brothers went bankrupt overnight, and President Bush had to invest $200 billion into AIG, because AIG guaranteed Freddie Mac loans held by foreign investors. The stock market fell from fourteen thousand to six thousand. Millions lost pension funds that had been saved for retirement, and stocks worth trillions were now worth no more than half their former value. Homes in hundreds of exclusive developments became almost worthless, and real estate values across the nation fell by forty percent, amounting to hundreds and hundreds of billions or trillions of dollars.

A CBS report on their Sunday evening program, "60 Minutes," showed houses being destroyed by the thousands in cities across the nation because they had been vacated by homeowners whose mortgage balance was more than the value of their homes. Also, cities are having to spend millions of dollars to destroy the houses. By one act, President Clinton became perhaps the biggest thief in history by stealing from upper and middle classes. By one act, he brought the net worth of the lower class, middle class, and upper class to a more common level. As Bastiat affirms, communist dictatorships begin by taking from the rich and giving to the poor. The world government of the Antichrist has already begun by making the rich poorer, and the poor richer. The end result will be to make all accountable to a central world economic system.

An *America's Money* report dated December 6, 2011, carried the headline: **"U.S. Falling Into Deeper Trouble, Faces 2013 Depression."** The article stresses that instead of recovering from the 2008 recession resulting from sub-prime mortgages of the Clinton years, the economy has steadily declined without any hope of recovery.

A CNN Money.com report dated October 25, 2011, carried the headline: **"Europe: Grimmer By the Minute."** This report stated that the debt limits of the European Union nations threatened the very existence of the European Union itself. There is also a call not only for a single European currency, but a world currency, as the base value of every nation's currencies presently change on a daily basis.

A Reuters report of October 24, 2011, was headlined: **"Vatican Calls for Global Authority on Economy."** The report stated in part:

> The Vatican called on Monday for the establishment of a "global public authority" and a "central world bank" to rule over financial institutions that have become outdated and often ineffective in dealing fairly with crises.
>
> The document from the Vatican's Justice and Peace department should please the "Occupy Wall Street" demonstrators and similar movements around the world who have protested against the economic downturn.

The prophet Daniel forewarned that in the last days when the government of Antichrist would appear, knowledge would increase and many would run to and fro. Rapid transportation and instant communication have reduced the world into a small ball in comparison to what it was even a thousand years ago. There is a growing demand for a world banking authority and a common monetary unit. It is only a matter of time before this becomes a reality. Even the Catholic Church, with its international institutions, is demanding such a single authority, and labels the difference in wages and living situations a sin. The fact that union workers in the United States earn twenty-five dollars an hour, while workers in China and India (who now produce what we drive, wear, eat, or sit on) make less than a dollar an hour is an imbalance that must be reconciled in the future. From a realistic economic position, the only answer is a world money authority and a world industrial and market authority. The Bible foretells the answer: a central authority over all money and every worker on a basic salary. In order to fit into such a world economic system, everyone must have a number or some international membership identification.

Several years ago, I wrote a paper entitled "Your Chinese Neighbor Next Door." Now we not only have a Chinese neighbor next door (communications and industrially speaking), we also have Muslim, Hindu, Buddhist, and neighbors of every race, religion, and political affiliation living next door. And, the world continues to get smaller every day. How can Americans adjust to this new interdependent world relationship?

> And he had power to give life unto the image of the beast, that the image of the beast should both speak, and cause that as many as would not worship the image of the beast should be killed. And he causeth all, both small and great,

rich and poor, free and bond, to receive a mark in their right hand, or in their foreheads: And that no man might buy or sell, save he that had the mark, or the name of the beast, or the number of his name. Here is wisdom. Let him that hath understanding count the number of the beast: for it is the number of a man; and his number is Six hundred threescore and six. —Revelation 13:15–18

Spirit of Antichrist in Today's Church

Jesus Christ is God's Messiah. Antichrist is Satan's messiah. Satan cannot create; he can and does counterfeit what God has created. Jesus Christ established His church. Antichrist is presently forming his church. That the nucleus, the main apostles of Antichrist, will come out of apostate Christendom is evidenced in the following scriptures:

> . . . when the Son of man cometh, shall he find faith on the earth? —Luke 18:8

> Even him, whose coming is after the working of Satan with all power and signs and lying wonders, And with all deceivableness of unrighteousness in them that perish; because they received not the love of the truth, that they might be saved. —2 Thessalonians 2:9–10

> Now the Spirit speaketh expressly, that in the latter times some shall depart from the faith, giving heed to seducing spirits, and doctrines of devils.
> —1 Timothy 4:1

And it was given unto him to make war with the saints, and to overcome them: and power was given him over all kindreds, and tongues, and nations. And all that dwell upon the earth shall worship him, whose names are not written in the book of life of the Lamb slain from the foundation of the world. —Revelation 13:7-8

And I beheld another beast coming up out of the earth; and he had two horns like a lamb, and he spake as a dragon.... And he doeth great wonders, so that he maketh fire come down from heaven on the earth in the sight of men, And deceiveth them that dwell on the earth by the means of those miracles . . . and cause that as many as would not worship the image of the beast should be killed.
—Revelation 13:11, 13-15

... I saw a woman sit upon a scarlet coloured beast, full of names of blasphemy.... And the woman was arrayed in purple and scarlet colour, and decked with gold and precious stones and pearls, . . . And upon her forehead was a name written, MYSTERY, BABYLON THE GREAT, THE MOTHER OF HARLOTS AND ABOMINATIONS OF THE EARTH. And I saw the woman drunken with the blood of the saints, and with the blood of the martyrs of Jesus.... How much she hath glorified herself, and lived deliciously, so much torment and sorrow give her: for she saith in her heart, I sit a queen, and am no widow, and shall see no sorrow.
—Revelation 17:3-6; 18:7

And the ten horns [ten national leaders] . . . shall hate

the whore, and shall make her desolate and naked, and shall eat her flesh, and burn her with fire. For God hath put in their hearts to fulfil his will. . . . —Revelation 17:16–17

The composite picture of the visible church (and when we say visible church, we mean all whose names are on a church roll) is as follows:

Jesus indicated that at the time of His Second Coming, faith in Him as the Christ of God will be practically nonexistent. On my latest (fifty-fourth) tour to Israel, 99.8 percent of the Jewish population still did not believe that Jesus Christ was their Messiah. Jewish children in Israel are still taught in school that Jesus was responsible for the destruction of the Temple and Jerusalem, and it is because of Jesus that they have been scattered and persecuted in all nations for the past two thousand years. However, the time is near, as we read in Revelation 1:7, that when the remnant of Israel personally sees the nail prints in His hands, they will know and accept Him as the Messiah. But Jesus spoke of a time just prior to His unveiling to the Jewish remnant. According to the second chapter of 2 Thessalonians, the majority of the memberships of the denominations will be comprised of people who have been deceived by the lie of Antichrist. The lie of Antichrist is defined in 1 John 4:3: ". . . every spirit that confesseth not that Jesus Christ is come in the flesh . . . is that spirit of antichrist. . . ." All concur that Jesus came in the flesh as an actual historical figure, but only a minority of church members today confess that Jesus Christ came in the flesh as God incarnate. There is a vast difference. Most accept Jesus as a good man, a great teacher, or a religious leader, but they do not accept Him as the Messiah of

God, the Christ, who died for our sins. This is the spirit of antichrist working in the churches of our day to convert them into churches for Antichrist. The Scriptures plainly indicate that this mass of apostate Christendom will become Antichrist's church during the Tribulation period.

That the Antichrist will have his church is a fact of Scripture. In the thirteenth chapter of Revelation, God's Word states that this church will bring all the world to worship the beast, the world dictator, as God. This church will have an ecclesiastical head identified as the False Prophet, who seemingly duplicates the work of the Holy Spirit in performing miracles, and he seemingly duplicates the work of the Holy Spirit at Pentecost by bringing fire down from Heaven. It will be a militant and revolutionary church—causing all who refuse to worship Antichrist as the Messiah to have their heads cut off.

In Revelation 17, the church of Antichrist is described as an overdressed harlot, filled with the blood of the Tribulation saints. Her name is related to the evil religious system of Revelation 2:20, called Jezebel. Jezebel was the harlot wife of King Ahab, who filled Israel with temple prostitutes. She killed everyone who identified themselves with Jehovah and refused to worship her false god. She even temporarily overcame God's servant Elijah, and the frightened prophet fled southward as fast as he could go to the wilderness. It is our understanding of Scripture that Elijah fled to Petra to escape Jezebel, and this is where the faithful remnant of Israel will flee in order to escape the wrath of the Jezebel of the Tribulation, the church of Antichrist, whose headquarters will be in Jerusalem.

However, Elijah came back and overcame the harlot Jezebel, and Elijah is coming back also during the Tribulation, as we are informed in Malachi 4:5: "Behold, I will send you Elijah the prophet before the coming of the great and dreadful day of the LORD." Elijah will be one of the two witnesses mentioned in Revelation 11, and this great prophet of God will wrestle with that harlot Jezebel religious system, the Antichrist church, during the Tribulation, just as he fought wicked Jezebel in Israel of old times.

In Revelation 18, the Antichrist church is depicted as the fornicator. The harlot is described as having an illicit affair with the beast kingdom. The explanation of Scripture is that the church, that is, the body of Christ (all born-again believers) is espoused to Jesus Christ (2 Corinthians 11:2). The spiritual union of the church and Jesus Christ will occur at the translation and resurrection, called the Rapture, described in 1 Thessalonians 4:13–18. This spiritual marriage involves a uniting for life, as in an earthly marriage, but because Jesus Christ has eternal life, His bride, the members of His body, will also have eternal life. As the Scripture declares, ". . . and so shall we ever be with the Lord."

All who are saved at that time will be caught up, in a moment, to meet the Lord in the air. The unsaved, including those whose names are on the church roll but not in the Lamb's book of life, will be left behind. Or, as we read in 1 Thessalonians 5:3, "For when they [the unsaved] shall say, Peace and safety; then sudden destruction cometh upon them, as travail upon a woman with child; and they [the unsaved] shall not escape."

The unsaved mass within the many denominations will not be included in the marriage union with Jesus Christ. They will be left behind. They will, like the jilted bride, be left waiting at the altar. The millions of church members left behind will still constitute an organization; however, the organization will have no head. Therefore, when the Antichrist presents himself as a messiah, the false church immediately claims him as its spiritual husband.

When Jesus Christ appears for the true church at the Rapture, Christians are promised a glorified body like unto His glorified body. But the unsaved church members will be left behind with their same old bodies of flesh that are susceptible to sin, sickness, sorrow, and death. Therefore, the Antichrist and the False Prophet heap riches upon the harlot, and we read in Revelation 18:7, "How much she hath glorified herself. ..." The cheap imitation of glorification is no protection against the beast kingdom when the leaders of the empire grow tired of her, and, like most kept women, cast her aside.

The Antichrist church of the Tribulation is described as being composed of a world congregation of bloodthirsty fanatics, who have been deceived by the devil's lie—that Jesus Christ, while a good man, was not God in the flesh who offered atonement for sin. This world church, operating under the authority of the political and military power of Antichrist, will cause all the rest of the world to worship the "man of sin" as God, or be killed by beheading. Paul and John both bring out emphatically that the forming of the Tribulation church takes place at the end of the Church Age just prior to the Tribulation period. It is formed through the spirit of antichrist working in the churches of the last days, to lead men to believe a lie, that Jesus was the son of Mary and Joseph, but not God's only begotten Son who died for the sins of the world.

No poll has been taken, that we know of, concerning the basic doctrinal beliefs of church members in the United States.

A poll was taken in 1967 of delegates to a National Council of Churches (NCC) convention at Miami Beach, Florida. Admittedly, delegates from churches belonging to denominations affiliated with the NCC would be more liberal and agnostic in their beliefs concerning basic Christian doctrine. But even so, the results of the poll, as reported in the July 1967 edition of *Christianity Today,* were astounding. Most of the delegates were ordained ministers of the Christian message and faith, yet one-third could not ascribe to a belief in God. Seventy-five percent of the delegates did not believe that the miracles recorded in the Bible were really miracles. Eighty-seven percent rejected the cardinal teaching of the Scriptures that man is born in sin. Seventy-nine percent expressed the opinion that salvation depended more on racial tolerance and love of fellowman, than on a personal faith in Jesus Christ as Savior. *Christianity Today* also reported that the consensus of NCC delegates at the convention was that non-Christians have just as much hope for salvation as members of Christian churches. By Bible definition, this is a manifestation of the spirit of antichrist in the churches, a movement that will eventually subvert the visible churches and make them an instrument for Satan's use. This warning and stern exhortation is set forth in 2 John, verses 7, 10–11:

> ... many deceivers are entered into the world, who confess not that Jesus Christ is come in the flesh. This is a deceiver and an antichrist.... If there come any unto you, and bring not this doctrine, receive him not into your house, neither bid him God speed: For he that biddeth him God speed is partaker of his evil deeds.

We again point out that the Scripture is not referring to the denial of Jesus as a historical figure, but rather that He was, and is, the Christ of God, the only Name under Heaven whereby men must be saved. Thus, the greatest evidence of the spirit of antichrist rising to the full in the last days, as far as the church is concerned, is the membership at large denying that Jesus is the Christ. Church leaders, for the most part, have turned from the glorious Gospel to declare a social gospel, or the gospel of revolution.

Occultism

The second manifestation of antichrist working within the realm of Christendom in the last days is the weakening influence of the Holy Spirit upon the world through the carnality of believers, making way for a latter-day invasion of demons and evil spirits: "... the Spirit [Holy Spirit] speaketh expressly, that in the latter times some shall depart from the faith, giving heed to seducing spirits, and doctrines of devils" (1 Tim. 4:1). Newspapers and religious publications are filled with articles concerning demonism and Satan worship. Many theologians suggested this was merely a fad that would pass in time. However, instead of declining, involvement in the occult continues to increase. The February 4, 1976, edition of the *Daily Oklahoman* carried the following article in the headline "Occultism Spreading":

> Serious occultism has not peaked out, but is actually gaining wider acceptance in America . . . said Dr. Lynn McMillin of Oklahoma Christian College. . . . Speaking during Religious

Emphasis Week at Central State University, McMillin told an audience ... that an estimated 20 million Americans are actively engaged in practicing, analyzing or reading about occultism.... He said he defined an occultist as one who makes use of supposed mystical power such as that involved in astrology, fortune telling, spiritualism, magic, witchcraft, Satanism and demonism.... The resurgence ... seems to represent an alternate form of reality as opposed to traditional scientific and religious outlook of western society.

This educator sees the continued increase of Satanism and demonism as evidence that Western civilization, based on faith in Jesus Christ, is crumbling. This is a sign of the spirit of antichrist bringing in the mystery of iniquity that is to precede the unveiling of the "man of sin."

The fastest growing of all the modern occult groups is the so-called "New Age movement." This coalition of occult organizations has sponsored ads in major magazines and newspapers around the world to announce that the "Christ" is coming. The basic doctrine of this religion is that there have been many masters like Jesus, Buddha, Mohammed, etc., but only one Christ. They say their messiah is coming soon to lead mankind into an evolutionary new age. *Omni,* one of the leading magazines of the eighties, in an article on the New Age movement in its July 1984 edition, quoted one of the sect's leaders, Robert Monroe: "Man is approaching a window of opportunity.... By expanding his consciousness, he has the chance to make a quantum jump in evolution. **Those who don't convert to man-plus will become phased out...."**

Revolution

The basic precept of Christianity, as far as the political structure of the world is concerned, is that when Jesus Christ returns, He will bring in His Kingdom from Heaven, and the government will be upon His own shoulders (Isaiah 9:6). But in these last days, even the non-Catholic churches have become involved in changing the world through political action. The World Council of Churches (WCC) at its 1966 convention in Geneva dedicated itself to the concept of world change through revolution. The 1966 WCC Conference Report read in part: "Rationalization of distribution . . . under the auspices of the United Nation . . . elimination of the adverse effect of price fluctuations and terms of trade . . . the establishment of world commodity marketing boards . . . an international division of labor . . . a system of international taxation."

Barron's, a national weekly recognized as one of the most respected financial publications of its kind, stated in a January 1967 edition:

> How many millions of people would be dislocated, ruined, enslaved, tortured, and murdered under a World Council of Churches' plan to restructure the world economy? . . . Was any past crime committed in the name of Christianity during the darkest ages of history of greater magnitude than that contemplated in the World Council of Churches?

Quoting next from an article by columnist Patrick J. Buchanan that appeared in the January 27, 1976, edition of the *Daily Oklahoman:*

Malcolm Muggeridge wrote in *Jesus Rediscovered,* "I have come to regard clerical Christianity and its officers as farcical." Watching the delegates of the World Council of Churches squabbling with one another... how best to damn western capitalism and avoid condemning religious repression in Russia, one knows whereof he speaks.

This newspaper columnist brings out that the WCC and the NCC have continued in their plans to make the United Nations a world government, and redistribute the wealth of the world, by force if necessary. We are told that the world religious establishment in the last days would be a cruel system, commanding everyone to worship Antichrist and take his mark, or they would not be able to eat. What is taking place within the visible ecumenical organizations indicates that Antichrist may indeed already be in the world.

The Purpose Driven Church Movement

The preceding part of this chapter, written in the mid-eighties, is just as relevant today as when it was written. Jesus warned that one of the most evident signs of the last days would be the rise of false christs and false prophets (Matthew 24:11).

Of course, Dr. Robert Schuller's ministry, centered at the Crystal Cathedral, has declined in scope, but in its place has risen one even more powerful and far-reaching and apostate, the Purpose Driven Church movement under its founder Dr. Rick Warren. The apostate teachings and outreach of the National Council of Churches and World Council of Churches opened the way for such a perverse religious deception, which further opens the way for the appearance of the antichrist religious system. Dr. Warren started the movement in Orange County, California, by starting the Saddleback Church for non-Christians. The Purpose Driven Church movement has taken over thousands of church properties and ministries throughout the nation.

The following article I wrote in our January 2009 edition of the *Prophetic Observer* will help explain to some extent the dangerous outreach of the Schuller/Warren apostasies.

Confusion in California

There are many outstanding Christians and patriotic citizens in California. Thousands of born-again Californians support this ministry. Yet, California also has more than its share of confused citizens—sexually, politically, and spiritually.

One such confused person is Dr. Robert Schuller, pretending to be a minister of Jesus Christ. Dr. Schuller has consistently presented a mixture of New Age, ecumenical, so-called positive thinking, and Eastern mysticism, but little basic Christian message. He stated in his autobiography, *My Journey:*

"I met once more with the Grand Mufti [a Muslim], truly one of the great Christ–honoring leaders of faith. . . . I'm dreaming a bold impossible dream: that positive-thinking believers in God will rise above the illusions that our sectarian religions have imposed on the world, and that leaders of the major faiths will rise above doctrinal idiosyncrasies, choosing not to focus on disagreements, but rather to transcend divisive dogmas to work together to bring peace and prosperity and hope to the world. Standing before a crowd of devout Muslims with the Grand Mufti, I know that we're all doing God's work together. Standing on the edge of a new millennium, we're laboring hand in hand to repair the breach."

It was announced this past month that Dr. Shuller's son, Robert Jr., who had taken his father's place in the church and on the national program for the past several years, was suddenly dismissed, the TV program not even airing his last national show. Robert Sr. announced that he and his son no longer shared the same vision for the ministry and that he was going to present outstanding men of faith in his son's place. What men of faith will Senior present, men like the Grant Mufti of Islam? Someone who is more informed about the ministry at Crystal Cathedral reported to us that Dr. Schuller's son fired the homosexuals on staff and was preaching a more basic, fundamental, evangelical message, which infuriated his father.

Almost within a stone's throw of the Crystal Cathedral is Dr. Rick Warren and his church, Saddleback. As brought out by Warren Smith, Roger Oakland, and others, the ministries of Dr. Warren and Dr. Schuller are much the same. As I have documented many times, Dr. Warren consistently criticizes those who hold to traditional fundamental Christian beliefs. The *Philadelphia Inquirer* of January 8, 2006, reported Dr. Warren as stating: "Fundamentalism of all varieties will be one of the big enemies of the 21st century: Muslim fundamentalism, Christian fundamentalism, Jewish fundamentalism, and secular fundamentalism." Also *Time* reported him as stating that to the church "you add Muslims, and add in Hindus, and all different religions, and you use all these houses of worship for distribution centers." There is no difference between Dr. Schuller and Dr. Warren on missions or doctrine.

The December 21, 2008, *Los Angeles Times* headlined a story, "**Pastor Rick Warren Addresses Muslim Group: Emphasizes Need to Find Common Ground.**" The only common ground, as far as faith and worship is concerned, that I have with a Muslim is that if he doesn't try to kill me, I won't try to kill him. Dr. Warren was given much credit for saying that marriage was between a man and a woman when Proposition 8 was an issue recently in California. Gays have criticized Obama for having Dr. Warren give the invocation at his inauguration simply because of his one statement about marriage. But quoting Dr. Warren from the article in the *Los Angeles Times,* as referenced above:

"From being tapped to deliver the invocation at President-elect Barack Obama's inauguration, Orange County Pastor Rick Warren spoke Saturday night to about 800 members of the Muslim Public Affairs Council at its convention in Long Beach. Warren's theme was about people getting along, forgetting their differences, and focusing on areas of agreement. The audience cheered him, and many people rose to their feet. Among the first to stand was singer Melissa Etheridge, a lesbian, who performed for the audience. Recognizing the potential for controversy, Warren said near the beginning of his speech, 'Let me just get this over very quickly. I love Muslims. And for the media's purposes, I happen to love gays and straights.'"

To me the two darkest areas of human existence are Islam and the homosexual lifestyle.

> "Be ye not unequally yoked together with unbelievers: for what fellowship hath righteousness with unrighteousness? and what communion hath light with darkness? And what concord hath Christ with Belial? or what part hath he that believeth with an infidel? . . . Wherefore come out from among them, and be ye separate, saith the Lord, and touch not the unclean thing; and I will receive you" (2 Corinthians 6:14–15, 17).

A Patriot Newswire report dated December 12, 2011, stated in part: "CHRISTIAN CHURCHES READ QURAN FROM PULPITS ACROSS AMERICA. . . . If this didn't happen to you . . . count yourself fortunate. It did happen . . . in churches across America." There is an interfaith movement, so-called, that intends to bring all churches together under a combination called "Christlam," which will encompass of course, the Purpose Driven Church movement. The Purpose Driven Church movement did take over my church in Oklahoma City, which grew from a mission in 1975 to the second largest Baptist Church in Oklahoma. Most of the membership left, leaving millions of dollars of church properties to the PDC owners. My book, *The Dark Side of the Purpose Driven Church*, and especially my tract, "Is Your Church Going Purpose Driven? How Can You Tell?" have saved some churches. If the reader would want either, he or she may call our office on weekdays—1-800-652-1114.

A person with a mean spirit commits mean acts. As prophesied, the spirit of antichrist is taking over the apostate church movements of our day and, supported by governments and a one-world news media, a world church is coming. But also according to prophecy, the False Prophet and the Antichrist will hate the whore and try to destroy it.

And where does the Catholic Church figure into this prophecy? At present, the Catholic Church is a bystander, waiting to pick up the pieces. But Malachi, who a thousand years ago prophesied the exact chronology of every pope, indicated the present pope is the next to the last pope. Under the next pope, Malachi prophesied, Rome would be destroyed. If Malachi's last prophecy comes to pass, it could be at this time that everyone who will not take the mark and number of the Antichrist, and worship him as God, will be beheaded (Revelation 20:4).

It may be noted that the method of execution used by Muslims is beheading. Will the Antichrist be a Muslim? Maybe yes, maybe no . . . but it is something to consider. Strong Muslim nations surround Israel, and the Muslims are in control of the Temple Mount upon which the Antichrist will commit the Abomination of Desolation.

We are living as Jesus warned, as in the days of Noah when God's authority is not only challenged but internationally rejected. We are also living as it was in the days of Lot, when moral degeneration is almost absolute. We cry for a revival in the churches, but the spirit of antichrist seems to be the guiding spirit.

Antichrist Influence in Nations Today

The prophetic Word of God declares without qualification that in the extremity of this age all nations will be joined together in a world empire, and the armies out of this empire will march against the armies of Jesus Christ at the Battle of Armageddon. The greatest army mankind has ever marshalled to this time will be under the command of Antichrist. This fact of prophetic history is set forth in the following scriptures:

> The kings of the earth set themselves . . . against the Lord, and against his anointed. . . . Thou shalt break them with a rod of iron. . . . —Psalms 2:2, 9

> And in the days of these kings shall the God of heaven set up a kingdom, which shall never be destroyed. . . .
> —Daniel 2:44

> Behold, the day of the Lord cometh. . . . I will gather all nations against Jerusalem to battle. . . . —Zechariah 14:1-2

> And the winepress was trodden without the city, and blood

came out of the winepress, even unto the horse bridles, by the space of a thousand and six hundred furlongs.
—Revelation 14:20

... They are the spirits of devils, working miracles which go forth unto the kings of the earth and of the whole world, to gather them to the battle of that great day of God Almighty. ... And he gathered them together into a place called in the Hebrew tongue Armageddon. —Revelation 16:14, 16

Beat your plowshares into swords, and your pruninghooks into spears.... Assemble yourselves, ... and the heavens and the earth shall shake.... —Joel 3:10–11, 16

And I saw heaven opened, and behold a white horse; and he that sat upon him.... And he was clothed with a vesture dipped in blood. ... And the armies which were in heaven followed him.... And out of his mouth goeth a sharp sword, that with it he should smite the nations: and he shall rule them with a rod of iron.... And he hath on his vesture and on his thigh a name written, KING OF KINGS, AND LORD OF LORDS. —Revelation 19:11–16

The foregoing scriptures, and many more, foretell that at the end of the age the spirit of antichrist will spread to all nations, ushering in a generation of war and armament races. Even the weaker nations will muster awesome weapons of destruction.

Proclaim ye this among the Gentiles; Prepare war, wake up the mighty men, let all the men of war draw near; let them come up: Beat your plowshares into swords, and your pruninghooks into spears: let the weak say, I am strong. Assemble yourselves, and come, all ye heathen, and gather yourselves together round about: thither cause thy mighty ones to come down, O Lord. Let the heathen be wakened, and come up to the valley of Jehoshaphat: for there will I sit to judge all the heathen round about. Put ye in the sickle, for the harvest is ripe: come, get you down; for the press is full, the fats overflow; for their wickedness is great. Multitudes, multitudes in the valley of decision: for the day of the Lord is near in the valley of decision. The sun and the moon shall be darkened, and the stars shall withdraw their shining. The Lord also shall roar out of Zion, and utter his voice from Jerusalem; and the heavens and the earth shall shake: but the Lord will be the hope of his people, and the strength of the children of Israel. So shall ye know that I am the Lord your God dwelling in Zion, my holy mountain: then shall Jerusalem be holy, and there shall no strangers pass through her any more. —Joel 3:9-17

The nations of the world, even the smaller nations, are preparing and arming for this day. The nations that have nuclear weapons today, and how many, are as follows:

- **China:** 100–200 warheads
- **France:** approximately 350 strategic warheads
- **Russia:** 2,787 strategic warheads, approximately 2,000 operational tactical warheads, and approximately 8,000 stockpiled strategic and tactical warheads

- » **United Kingdom:** less than 160 deployed strategic warheads
- » **United States:** 2,126 strategic warheads, approximately 500 operational tactical weapons, and approximately 6,700 reserve strategic and tactical warheads
- » **India:** up to 100 nuclear warheads
- » **Israel:** between 75 and 200 nuclear warheads
- » **Pakistan:** between 70 and 90 nuclear warheads

In addition to these nations, there are others like North Korea, Iran, and Syria that have nuclear weapons, or are attempting to develop them. The spring 2011 revolutions in the Muslim nations of the Middle East are bringing these nations together to destroy Israel.

As prophesied in the eleventh chapter of Daniel, the nations will be divided into four main blocs—the king of the west, the king of the north, the kings of the east, and the king of the south. Israel will increasingly become a center of world controversy. A temporary peace arrangement will be entered into for a seven-year period, but after three and a half years, the treaty will be broken when the Antichrist appears in the Temple in Jerusalem and claims to be the real Messiah. After another three and a half year period of desolation and tribulation under the world dictatorship of Antichrist, the armies of all nations will be gathered into the Middle East to prevent the return of Jesus Christ to establish His Kingdom over the earth from Jerusalem. The outcome of this battle is already recorded in Scripture, but the point of interest for us today is how the events leading up to Armageddon are shaping up in our time. Behind this mad scheme to arm the nations with weapons of annihilation such as the world has never witnessed, and amass them in Israel to prevent the return of Jesus Christ, is Satan's own false anointed messiah, the Antichrist. If there are signs that we are now witnessing the last stages of Satan's plan to prepare the nations for Armageddon, then there are sufficient reasons to conclude that the Antichrist may be in the world at this present hour.

While the mouthings of national and international representatives may appear to be matters of political, economic, or defense interests, behind the scenes is the plan of Satan to eventually destroy Israel and prevent Jesus Christ from returning to establish a Millennial Kingdom.

Arming the Nations

Statistics indicate that half of all the casualties of war since the recorded history of mankind (approximately six thousand years) have occurred within the past ninety years, yet the world armament race continues. In World War I, there were almost 8.5 million military casualties, and 1.35 million civilian casualties. In World War II, there were approximately 17 million military casualties, and over 34 million civilians dead. In addition, there were the Spanish civil war, the China civil war, the Korean war, the Vietnam war, a multitude of wars in Africa and Central America, war in Afghanistan, four major wars in the Middle East involving Israel, the Lebanese civil war, the Iraq-Iran war, and dozens of smaller wars over the face of the globe.

Advanced conventional weapons, as well as atomic and hydrogen weapons, have made even small nations fearsome aggressors. It is as we read in Joel 3:10, "Beat your plowshares into swords, and your pruninghooks into spears: let the weak say, I am strong."

The June 1975 edition of *Reader's Digest* announced the fulfillment of Joel's prophecy in an article titled "Weapons For All Nations," which stated in part:

> Like a self-inflicted plague, international trade in arms is sweeping across the world with epidemic force.... Nowhere is the boom in arms sales more apparent than in the Persian Gulf.... Iran has spent about $8 billion in the United States alone, requiring one of the world's most modern arsenals. ... Their army boasts (besides hundreds of the latest war planes) 3,000 armored vehicles and more than 1,000 helicopters.... Iraq has bought MiG fighters, heavy artillery, and surface-to-surface missiles, which can be fitted with nuclear warheads, from the Soviets. Saudi Arabia is buying planes, tanks, attack helicopters and coastal-defense vessels.... Even tiny Abu Dhabi...has obtained Mirage [fighter planes].

We read also from an article that appeared in the January 1, 1975, edition of the *Kansas City Star* entitled "Whole World a Hostage":

> Middle Eastern countries are now armed at a level that equals or surpasses the traditionally strong European powers. Israel, Egypt, Syria, and Iran have more powerful ... forces than, for example, West Germany, Britain, France and Italy.... Everyone has suspected for years that Israel was in a position to fight a nuclear war.... It is an astounding

paradox that countries with relatively small industrial infrastructures and often with tiny populations can represent such martial threats.

In 1952, the total international arms traffic amounted to only $300 million. In 1975, it had risen to $20 billion. And although we have no current statistics, we would estimate that international arms sales now exceed $100 billion a year. In the eighties we were at Aqaba in Jordan, and there was a steady stream of trucks carrying Soviet armaments through Amman to Syria. The Jordanian side of the Gulf of Aqaba is clogged with Russian ships.

No longer are the Apocalypse and Armageddon used in symbolic terms; almost every newscast and newspaper edition uses both words literally. *Time* magazine recently observed: "Waiting for Armageddon is, in a curious way, one of the morbidly titillating preoccupations of our time . . . in the apocalyptic imagination."

An estimated sixty thousand nuclear bombs are currently allocated throughout the continents and oceans of the world, and ten new ones are being made every day. According to a report by John Wesley White on page 25 of *Arming for Armageddon,* a crashing B-52 bomber jettisoned two nuclear bombs over Goldsboro, North Carolina. One bomb broke apart on impact, but the parachute carrying the second bomb got caught in a tree. Five of the six interlocking safety switches were released. If the sixth switch had been triggered, a bomb eighteen hundred times more powerful than the one dropped on Hiroshima would have exploded. The November 28, 1983, edition of *U.S. News & World Report* observed:

More than at any time since the depth of the cold war, public attention is being focused on nuclear conflict by the spate of TV programs and movies dramatizing an atomic holocaust. . . . If war comes, it would not be with a single enormous explosion, but with deadly cadence of blasts spread out over many minutes, possibly even days or weeks. There would be time for many to die of fear.

Jesus said of the time of His return: "Men's hearts failing them for fear, and for looking after those things which are coming on the earth: for the powers of heaven shall be shaken" (Luke 21:26).

Four Blocs of Nations

According to chapters 9 and 11 of Daniel, Ezekiel 38, and Revelation 16:12, there will be four blocs of nations in the world before they are solidified into one empire under the reign of Antichrist. These four blocs of nations are to become more godless in nature as the Great Tribulation approaches. This is evident from our study on the influence of antichrist on the churches of today. But let us consider these blocs of nations one by one:

King of the South (Daniel 11:40)

The one thing that all four blocs of nations will have in common is they will all be anti-Israel and, in the final analysis, anti-God. The African nations voted together to condemn Israel in the United Nations as a racist nation. The continent of Africa, geographically located to the south of Jerusalem, God's central compass point, comprises 20 percent of the Earth's landmass. Of the 350 million population of the nations of Africa, 9 percent are identified with the three divisions of Christendom (Catholic, Protestant, and Eastern Orthodox). The remaining 91 percent of non-Christian Africans are mostly adherents of the Muslim faith or the Hindu religion.

Egypt is identified in Scripture in its traditional political position as the king of the south. Israel is vehemently attacked in the Egyptian press, which is controlled by the government. Libya and Ethiopia are identified in Ezekiel 38 as members of the alliance led by Russia that will attack Israel in the last days. Both nations are exceedingly hostile toward Israel. The only real friend that Israel has in Africa today is the Union of South Africa.

King of the North (Daniel 11:40)

According to Ezekiel 38, in the latter times when Israel would be refounded as a nation, a powerful anti-God nation would rise up to the north of Jerusalem. This nation, with all its allies, is the king of the north. This powerful nation is called Gog, and identified by its two principal cities, Meshech (Moscow) and Tubal (Tobolsk). Russia is today often called Gog in the Israeli newspapers. Russia and communist satellites of Eastern Europe are violently anti-Israel and anti-God. This bloc of nations comprises approximately 25 percent of the earth's landmass and about 12 percent of the world's population.

Kings of the East (Revelation 16:12)

This bloc of anti-God nations is described in Revelation 16:12, "And the sixth angel poured out his vial upon the great river

Euphrates; and the water thereof was dried up, that the way of the kings of the east might be prepared."

The Apostle John, as noted in Revelation 9:13–16, heard the number of the army from the east that would cross the Euphrates on the way to Armageddon, and it was "two hundred thousand thousand," or 200 million men. Communist China has boasted that the nation could field an army of 200 million—the exact figure given in Scripture. The direction is right, the number is right, and the nation's attitude toward God corresponds to the Scripture. Also, due to the completion of the Tabqa Dam across the Euphrates River in Syria, for the first time in history the Euphrates can be dried up as the prophecy states. But the spirit of antichrist in communist China has swept to the south on the Asian continent, bringing another bloc of nations comprising 20 percent of the landmass of earth, and approximately 50 percent of the world's population under anti-God regimes.

North Korea, Vietnam, Cambodia, and Laos now have communist governments that are avowed enemies of Israel.

King of the West (Daniel 9:26)

Daniel 9:26 and other scriptures indicate a revival of the Roman Empire in the form of a ten-nation alliance within the old Roman boundaries in Western Europe. When the headquarters for the Common Market was erected in Brussels, ten flagpoles were erected in front of the building for the flags from ten nations. Today, the number in the Common Market alliance has increased to twenty-seven. Scripture indicates that it is out of the western nations that the Antichrist will appear. This is also logical in light of the growing apostasy of the churches in Europe and the United States, because it will be apostate Christendom, after true Christians are caught up to be with the Lord, that will cause all the world to worship this "man of sin" as God. The continued moral decline, along with worsening economic and political conditions of the western nations, indicates that such an event may not be too far in the future. Thus, we see all four blocs of nations ready to assume their role in prophecy under the reign of Antichrist.

Mr. President of Planet Earth

In recent years, there have appeared several books about planet Earth. Most of these books have been written on a negative note: *Good-bye Planet Earth, The Late Great Planet Earth*, etc. But according to God's Word, there are many things yet to happen to earth before the Creator is through with it. One of the events that lies in the future is that earth will have a president all its own. It is no coincidence that the July 1, 1974, edition of *Time* magazine carried the following suggestion: "Kissinger's achievements have, at last, justified the establishment of a new political office, which I sincerely hope the United Nations will consider: President of planet earth."

We do not say that Henry Kissinger is a future world dictator, the Antichrist; however, he has created the desire in some quarters for such a world office. Arnold Toynbee predicted in his twelve-volume edition of *The History of Man* that the nations would have a ruthless dictatorship in the near future. James Orwell, in his book *Nineteen Eighty-Four*, predicted a world dictatorship by this date. Catholic bishop Fulton Sheen has said that the Antichrist is coming *"disguised as a Great Humanitarian*—he will talk peace, prosperity and plenty. . . ."

Newspaper editorial writers point out almost daily that the world is looking for a messiah, a man with all the answers to the energy, food, and population problems of our time. Dr. Vance Havner, the noted evangelist, said: "The real issue today is not Russia or the atom bomb, as important as they are. The issue is Christ or Antichrist—God who became man, or the man who will claim to be God."

In Isaiah 28:5 the Lord at His coming is pictured as a "diadem of beauty." The prophet also wrote in Isaiah 33:17 to those who will be alive on earth when Jesus Christ returns: "Thine eyes shall see the king in his beauty. . . ." Jesus said, ". . . If I go and prepare a place for you, I will come again . . ." (John 14:3).

The proposition for the world today is not, "If Christ comes back," but rather, "When is He coming back?" Likewise, inasmuch as Jesus will meet the Antichrist and the armies of this world in battle at Armageddon, the second proposition is not, "If Antichrist comes," but rather, "How near is his coming?" The influence of antichrist over the nations today indicates that he may be on the world scene. This frightening possibility should press a decision upon every man and woman at this present hour: Christ or Antichrist? Beauty or the Beast?

As we advance into the second decade of the twenty-first century, a new prophetic phenomena is developing—the international news media. Even in George Washington's day it could take months, or even years, for news about what was happening in Russia or China to reach the president. Daniel said that in the end of the age knowledge would increase; people would run to and fro; and John said that all the world would worship the image of the beast. All this is made possible by international television and the Internet. Within minutes all the world knows what is happening on any spot of the globe. All the world is made instantly aware of the terrible world disasters that occurred in 2011, including earthquakes, tornadoes, plagues, famines, and economic woes. The news media magnifies the bad news of disasters and world problems, rather than focusing on the positive. The propaganda is that now we must have a central authority and a central government to handle all these disasters and problems.

The Antichrist will appear claiming to have the answers to all these problems, and as we read in Revelation 13:8, all whose names are not written in the book of life will almost instantly worship this person called the beast. Is that world leader alive today? The signs of our time indicate that he very well could be.

The Antichrist System

In the previous eight chapters of our study, *Is the Antichrist Alive Today?*, we have discussed the influence of the coming antichrist system on the various divisions of our present-day, economy, the church, the financial structure, and the political status. However, the entire system is depicted as emanating from one central source of evil, Satan, also called the Dragon and Leviathan in the Bible. Both names for the satanic system mean the same. The crumbling of the system is foretold in Revelation 12:9: "And the great dragon was cast out, that old serpent, called the Devil, and Satan, which deceiveth the whole world: he was cast out into the earth, and his angels were cast out with him."

The first book of the Bible to be written is the Book of Job, and the first chapter of the first book of Scripture to be penned establishes two facts: The existence of God, and the existence of Satan:

> Now there was a day when the sons of God [angels] came to present themselves before the LORD, and Satan came also among them. And the LORD said unto Satan, Whence comest thou? Then Satan answered the LORD, and said, From going to and fro in the earth, and from walking up and down in

it. And the LORD said unto Satan, Hast thou considered my servant Job, that there is none like him in the earth, a perfect and an upright man, one that feareth God, and escheweth evil? Then Satan answered the LORD, and said, Doth Job fear God for nought? —Job 1:6–9

As in the Book of Hosea, the central character of the book of Job acts out a prophetic account of things to come in real-life drama. God allowed Satan to inflict every kind of sorrow, tribulation, and suffering upon righteous Job, short of taking his life, to prove in the divine court of justice that this man would remain faithful and worthy of citizenship in God's eternal Kingdom. What happened to Job in real life is a type of what would happen to mankind down through the ages under Satan's attempt to accuse the human race before God as unworthy of being saved. In the Book of Job, Satan's coming messiah, the Antichrist, is also prophesied in type in great detail. For example, Job 18:11–18:

> Terrors shall make him afraid on every side, and shall drive him to his feet. His strength shall be hungerbitten, and destruction shall be ready at his side. It shall devour the strength of his skin: even the firstborn of death shall devour his strength. His confidence shall be rooted out of his tabernacle, and it shall bring him to the king of terrors. It shall dwell in his tabernacle, because it is none of his: brimstone shall be scattered upon his habitation. His roots shall be dried up beneath, and above shall his branch be cut off. His remembrance shall perish from the earth, and he shall

have no name in the street. He shall be driven from light into darkness, and chased out of the world.

We are informed by the Apostle Paul in 1 Corinthians 15:23 that Jesus Christ is the firstfruits, or the firstborn, of the first resurrection. Revelation 20:6 says, "Blessed and holy is he that hath part in the first resurrection: on such the second death hath no power...." The first resurrection encompasses the resurrection of the saved of all ages up to the time when Christ returns to bring in the Kingdom of Heaven upon rebel planet Earth. But we notice in Job 18:13 that the evil personage spoken of who would come, would be the "firstborn of death." This wicked one, the Antichrist, will be the firstborn of the second resurrection, the resurrection of the lost dead, Satan's false messiah. This prophetic passage in Job once more illustrates that the Antichrist will be of the living dead, an individual who has lived before. The devil's lie of reincarnation will be perpetrated upon a world looking for a super-ruler, and the devil will give unregenerate masses the super deceiver. The Scripture indicates he will be an individual who once lived, died, went into perdition (the bottomless pit), and came back to receive the crown of this world which Satan offered to Jesus Christ. This conclusion is verified in Revelation 17:8: "The beast that thou sawest was, and is not; and shall ascend out of the bottomless pit, and go into perdition: and they that dwell on the earth shall wonder, whose names were not written in the book of life from the foundation of the world, when they behold the beast that was, and is not, and yet is."

The unsaved dead are now in Hades awaiting their time of resurrection (Revelation 20:11–15). The Antichrist will be, or is, if he is in the world today, the firstborn of the unsaved dead, those ordained to perdition. Inasmuch as the devil will have brought him forth from the dead in the resurrected body of the lost, we read in Revelation 19:20 that Jesus Christ will cast the Antichrist directly into the "lake of fire." Thus, the Antichrist and his cohort, the False Prophet, will be the first two of the lost dead to be cast into the eternal "lake of fire." The light shed on the resurrection of Antichrist out of perdition in the Book of Job, in conjunction with Revelation 19:20, causes us to wonder if the False Prophet also might be a lost person whom Satan will bring forth to cause fire to come down from heaven. Job tells us that the Antichrist will be "chased out of the world," and according to Revelation 19:20, this is exactly what will happen. Jesus Christ and the armies of Heaven will chase him out of his "tabernacle" in Jerusalem (Daniel 11:45), and "brimstone" shall become his habitation forever.

The Leviathan

It is remarkable that one of Antichrist's aliases in the Bible is Leviathan. He is presented in God's biblical pattern in the heavens in the constellation Cetus as the Dragon. The name of Leviathan was given to the Antichrist by the prophet Isaiah: "In that day the LORD with his sore and great and strong sword shall punish leviathan the piercing serpent, even leviathan that crooked serpent; and he shall slay the dragon that is in the sea" (Isaiah 27:1).

In analyzing this verse of Scripture, *The Student's Commentary* says, "The day of indignation will be the day of God's wrath against, and destruction of, Leviathan the Antichrist."

The forty-first chapter of the Book of Job is devoted entirely to Satan's end-time masterpiece under the name Leviathan. Some Bible commentaries have passed over this particular prophecy, noting it only as a poetical description of a large crocodile. However, it seems hardly possible that the Holy Spirit would inspire thirty-four verses about a water animal, and not a very handsome one at that. It is also obvious from a reading of the account in Job 41 that an animal far more vicious than a crocodile is under observation.

God asked Job about the Leviathan, "Will he make many supplications unto thee? will he speak soft words unto thee?" (Job 41:3). The Antichrist will appear on the scene as a polished diplomat, speaking soft words of peace. God next says to Job, "None is so fierce that dare stir him up . . ." (vs. 10). This blends with Revelation 13:4, ". . . Who is like unto the beast? who is able to make war with him?" Consider also these added descriptive remarks concerning Leviathan:

> Out of his mouth go burning lamps, and sparks of fire leap out. Out of his nostrils goeth smoke, as out of a seething pot or caldron. His breath kindleth coals, and a flame goeth out of his mouth. . . . His heart is as firm as a stone; yea, as hard as a piece of the nether millstone. . . . He laugheth at the shaking of a spear. . . . Upon the earth there is not his like. . . . He is a king over all the children of pride.
> —Job 41:19–21, 24, 29, 33–34

All the preceding descriptions of Leviathan in Job 41 relate to the personality and reign of Antichrist. But in verse 4 of the same chapter, God asks Job an intriguing question: "Will he [Leviathan] make a covenant with thee? . . ." The answer is yes. The Antichrist will make a covenant with Israel.

Covenant With Death

The covenant that Satan's man will make with the Jews will cover a seven-year period, during which time far-reaching changes are scheduled to occur in Palestine. Details of the treaty are set forth in Daniel 9:27: "And he shall confirm the covenant with many for one week: and in the midst of the week he shall cause the sacrifice and the oblation to cease, and for the overspreading of abominations he shall make it desolate, even until the consummation, and that determined shall be poured upon the desolate."

The covenant as related to Israel in Scripture means the covenant with Abraham giving the land of Canaan (Palestine) to his seed forever, as recorded in Genesis 17:7–8: "And I will establish my covenant between me and thee and thy seed after thee in their generations for an everlasting covenant, to be a God unto thee, and to thy seed after thee. And I will give unto thee, and to thy seed after thee, the land wherein thou art a stranger, all the land of Canaan, for an everlasting possession; and I will be their God."

God gave the land of Palestine to the seed of Abraham, and this is the right that the Jews are attempting to establish today, in their own strength. But a man described as "the prince that shall come" (Daniel 9:26) will be successful in negotiating a treaty arrangement between Israel and those attempting to take the land of Palestine away from the Jews (probably the Arab states). This "prince that shall come" is the same person spoken of by Jesus in John 5:43, "... if another shall come in his own name, him ye will receive."

There are several Greek words translated "another" in the English versions of the Bible. The two most frequently used in the original text are *allos* and *heteros*. *Allos* means "another of the same racial stock or genus." The second signifies "another of a totally different kind."

Jesus used *allos* in John 5:43. If Antichrist were to be a gentile, the word *heteros* would have been employed. It is also evident from Daniel 11:37 that the Antichrist will be Jewish, at least on his mother's side, because Jewish racial descent is determined by the mother, going all the way back to Genesis 3:15, the "seed of the woman."

Strange as it may seem, the Book of Psalms, usually considered as a source of praise and blessings from God, also contains much information about the greatest criminal the world will ever know. The fifty-fifth psalm discusses the fundamental relationship which will exist between Antichrist and the Jews: "The words of his mouth were smoother than butter, but war was in his heart: his words were softer than oil, yet were they drawn swords" (Psalm 55:21).

This bitter phrase will be uttered by the Jews when they come to understand they have placed their hopes for survival on the promises of a traitor like Judas who betrayed Jesus Christ. The leaders of Israel bribed Judas to betray Jesus, but now they in turn are the victims of the greatest betrayal in Jewish history. As Jesus warned in Matthew 24:15–21, all the Jews in Israel who refuse to accept the beast as the promised Messiah will have to flee for their lives. The breaking of the covenant is prophesied in Psalm 55:20, "He hath put forth his hands against such as be at peace with him: he hath broken his covenant." The entire fifty-fifth psalm should be read with the thought of the broken covenant in mind, accompanied by the idea of an internal program launched by the man whom the

Jews accepted as their own, one whom they trusted. Out of this suffering, a remnant will be saved when they turn to the true Messiah, the Lord Jesus Christ.

God looks upon the folly of Israel in the last days to escape the "time of Jacob's trouble" prophesied in Isaiah 28:14–18:

> Wherefore hear the word of the LORD, ye scornful men, that rule this people which is in Jerusalem. Because ye have said, We have made a covenant with death, and with hell are we at agreement; when the overflowing scourge shall pass through, it shall not come unto us: for we have made lies our refuge, and under falsehood have we hid ourselves: Therefore thus saith the Lord GOD, Behold, I lay in Zion for a foundation a stone, a tried stone, a precious corner stone, a sure foundation: he that believeth shall not make haste. Judgment also will I lay to the line, and righteousness to the plummet: and the hail shall sweep away the refuge of lies, and the waters shall overflow the hiding place. And your covenant with death shall be disannulled, and your agreement with hell shall not stand; when the overflowing scourge shall pass through, then ye shall be trodden down by it.

Daniel informs us that not all Jews will accept the covenant proposed by Antichrist, and these will be the ones who have to flee for their lives when the covenant is broken. And the prophet said the men who rule in Jerusalem at this time will seek to escape the coming judgment by making a covenant with Death and an agreement with Hell. As we have already brought out, this means that the covenant-maker, the Antichrist, will be one who has been resurrected from the dead and brought up out of Hell and Perdition. It is this satanic personality with whom Israel will make a covenant. But the covenant will not stand, and the scourge of desolation will sweep away those who have endorsed the agreement with Hell. Only those left in God's hiding place at Petra will be saved to inherit the promises of God's true covenant with Abraham.

The spirit of antichrist is working in the world today to bring forth the entire satanic system that will spread over all the earth with the signing of a covenant with Israel. This covenant will promise Israel that they will not be molested or their land invaded for a period of seven years. Of course, it is understood that Israel in return will have to make concessions. What these concessions will be remains to be seen, but in light of current political conditions in the Middle East, they would appear to be: (1) the return of all conquered Arab lands, and (2) the establishment of a homeland for the Palestinian refugees along the eastern boundary of Israel. These two prime objectives have been considered the base for the proposed Geneva Peace Convention in the Middle East. Of course, there are other concessions that will probably enter into the covenant, and these will be covered in a subsequent study.

We are not trying to forge present political conditions in the Middle East into an established prophetic mold that fits the end-time situation, because it should be obvious that little force is required. The number one objective for such a treaty outlined in prophecy is already in evidence at this immediate point in time—the right of Israel to the land of Palestine. The peace treaty itself is in evidence, because world leaders agree that unless a settlement is reached on Middle East problems, that area will light the spark that will ignite the conflagration that will probably destroy the world. Dr. Kissinger in the 1970s cast himself into this sea of troubled waters as a world savior.

Since the Kissinger efforts to negotiate a peace accord between Israel and the Muslim world that would involve a divided Israel, every U.S. president—Carter, Reagan, Bush, Clinton, Bush, and Obama—have injected their own efforts, but to no avail. What has prevented a treaty or covenant over the land that God gave Israel is that the Arab world does not want a two-state solution, because it would be a recognition of the revival of the nation of Israel. The Islamic religion will not recognize the right of a Jew to even a grain of sand or a blade of grass from this land, now occupied by Jews that have returned according to biblical prophecy. It will take a world personality with a super-plan to get both Israel and the Muslim world to agree to a contingent peace arrangement over the land. No political or religious personality today—even the pope—has been able to accomplish this.

The first important personal act of the Antichrist will be to get Israel to sign a covenant whereby this satanic personality will get Israel to trust their security in his hands. This will lead to his appearance in the rebuilt Temple to declare himself as the messiah and demand all the world worship him as God.

On a recent tour to Israel, my fifty-fourth, we visited the Temple Institute in Jerusalem. All Temple vessels and furnishings have been rebuilt and remade in the finest wood, silver, and gold. The priest's clothing, according to biblical specifications, is ready. The priests have been DNA tested to make sure they are descendants of Aaron. The only obstruction to rebuilding the Temple is that on the Temple Mount, a Muslim shrine, the Dome of the Rock, sits over the Holy of Holies, the rock where Abraham offered Isaac, and a Muslim mosque and other buildings are also nearby. There was hope expressed that some agreement could be arranged whereby the Temple construction could begin. But where?

Seventy years is generally agreed the length in years of one generation, and seventy years from the refounding of Israel as a nation will be 2018. This may be an important year in prophetic history.

According to Zechariah 12, in the last days Jerusalem will be a burdensome stone for all nations. The Vatican wants to internationalize Jerusalem, because, according to Catholic beliefs, Jerusalem belongs to the pope. Bitter political battles rage in the world's capitals over moving embassies to Jerusalem from Tel Aviv. The Antichrist will seemingly settle this controversy when he will sit in the Temple in Jerusalem, making to himself the claim that he is the god of all religions (2 Thessalonians 2:4).

The political and religious motivations that will bring this prophecy to pass are already in motion. These surfacing apocalyptic events constitute supportive evidence that the Antichrist may already be in the world today.

Antichrist—His Name and Nature

Most people are familiar with the well-known saying of William Shakespeare: "What's in a name? A rose by any other name would smell as sweet."

Perhaps a rose would smell as sweet if it were called a skunk; or perhaps Agnes would be just as ugly, or beautiful, as the case may be, if she were called Melody or Angeline. As far as modern man is concerned, names are simply for identification purposes, and this is one reason why that will be a relatively simple matter for people in the future to accept a number in place of their name. Columnist Bob Considine stated in his column of March 2, 1974: "All signs point to a day, perhaps not far off, when money will go out of style.... Computerization is already well on its way to completely revolutionizing the banking business. Your signature on a check is now as obsolete as the use of beeswax to seal a letter. That string of incomprehensible letters in the bottom left hand corner of the check is the real you."

So what's in a name? A series of numbers, in the future, will mean just as much, if not more. But such has not always been the case. In the Bible, and especially in the Old Testament, names were very important. Names indicated the election and calling of God, and future rewards and blessings. King David, in his own pride, to extend his power over Israel, numbered the people, and God convicted him that this was wrong, as we read in 2 Samuel 24:10, "And David's heart smote him after that he had numbered the people. And David said unto the LORD, I have sinned greatly in that I have done: and now, I beseech thee, O LORD, take away the iniquity of thy servant; for I have done very foolishly."

God forgave David, but what the king had done in numbering the people could not be undone, and so we read in 2 Samuel 24:15, "So the LORD sent a pestilence upon Israel from the morning even to the time appointed: and there died of the people from Dan even to Beersheba seventy thousand men."

Taking away a person's name and replacing it with a number is serious business with God, and the reason that God was angry with David and put the killing of seventy thousand men on his conscience was because what the king of Israel did was a type of what antichrist would do. It is recorded in Revelation 13:11–18 that the Antichrist system will attempt to number and mark every person in the world. We read of those who will be numbered and marked by Antichrist in Revelation 14:9–10:

> And the third angel followed them, saying with a loud voice, If any man worship the beast and his image, and receive his mark in his forehead, or in his hand, The same shall drink of the wine of the wrath of God, which is poured out without mixture into the cup of his indignation; and he shall be tormented with fire and brimstone in the presence of the holy angels, and in the presence of the Lamb.

What's in a name? God says in Revelation 2:17, "... To him that overcometh will I give to eat of the hidden manna, and will give him a white stone, and in the stone a new name written, which no man knoweth saving he that receiveth it."

God has a name reserved for every Christian. While only three of the angelic host are identified by name in the Bible (Michael, Gabriel, and Lucifer), it is likely that all the angels in the heavens are named. We read in Genesis 2:19 that the first thing that God did after He created Adam was to bring the animals to Adam to be given a name. This emphasizes the importance God places upon names. He wanted the beasts of the field, and even the fowls of the air, to be named. Names in the Old Testament indicated the individual's relationship to God. The name of Enoch means "dedicated," and Enoch walked with God. Abraham means "the father of a great multitude." Gideon means "a great warrior," and God did indeed have to encourage Gideon to live up to his name. Iscariot means "a man of murder." And we could continue indefinitely concerning the naming of men, and how the names of biblical characters projected their relationship to God and their role in His Kingdom. Three members of the exalted angelic host are named: Gabriel, Michael, and Lucifer (so called before his fall). Therefore, it is reasonable to assume that all the angels of God have names. And just as Lucifer became Satan, we may conclude that all the angels who followed him in the rebellion have anti-names.

The name Jesus means "Jehovah is salvation." Christ means "the anointed one," or "God's anointed." He was sent to declare the mercy and grace of God upon all who would receive Him as Lord and Savior. The promise concerning the Messiah in the Old Testament was that He would come, not in His own name, but in the name of the Lord. We read in Psalm 118:22–28, "The stone which the builders refused is become the head stone of the corner.... Save now, I beseech thee, O LORD... Blessed be he that cometh in the name of the LORD.... God is the LORD, which hath shewed us light.... Thou art my God...."

When Jesus Christ entered Jerusalem to present His claim to David's throne, the multitude went before Him shouting: ". . . Hosanna [which means 'save us'] to the son of David: Blessed is he that cometh in the name of the Lord; Hosanna in the highest" (Matthew 21:9).

But the majority of Israel replied: "We will not have this man to rule over us," and Jesus said again in Matthew 23:38–39: "Behold, your house [the Temple] is left unto you desolate. For I say unto you, Ye shall not see me henceforth, till ye shall say, Blessed is he that cometh in the name of the Lord."

Not until Israel as a nation is willing to receive Jesus Christ as the Christ of God, the One who came into the world from God the Father, will He come back. And we are told in Zechariah 12:11–12 that Israel will look upon this One whom they have pierced—nailed to the cross—and they will receive Him as Savior, Lord, and King. But before Israel realizes the true identity of the Messiah, they will be deceived into accepting a false christ.

Concerning the name of the Antichrist, Jesus made an interesting remark as recorded in John 5:43: "I am come in my Father's name, and ye receive me not: if another shall come in his own name, him ye will receive."

The names of biblical characters, especially those of Jewish descent, related to a concise history of the individual, as we have already brought out. God's plan and purpose for Israel is that the people of the nation should be a blessing to all nations—in art, in politics, in government, in music, in medicine, etc. God's promise to Abraham, the father of multitudes, was "in thy seed shall all nations be blessed." Some may disagree with us, but it is our concerted opinion, as indicated in Scripture and confirmed by history, that God has given the Jewish race talents far above those of any other race. Not long ago a book was published giving statistics of the ratios of the members of each race in arts, crafts, government, and science. The number of Jews excelling in music, literature, medicine, science, finance, education, law, etc., outnumber all other races (according to population) more than two to one. Now here is a race of people, scattered throughout the nations for almost two thousand years, downtrodden, often without any civil rights whatsoever, and very limited educational opportunities, yet they have excelled above all other races in almost every field of human endeavor. There is a reason, and it goes back to God choosing the seed of Abraham to take His message, and His will and blessings, to all races, tongues, and kindreds.

This does not mean that all Jews are good people. There are wicked Jews just as there are wicked gentiles. However, because the Jews are usually smarter and more intelligent, whereas a gentile may go out and rob a service station of a few hundred dollars, a Jew, or a delegation of Jews, will take over a company, a city, or a nation, and do it all legally. Apart from God, the talents and intelligence of the Jews have often been a curse instead of a blessing. Also, in many cases, a Jew who has departed from the faith of Abraham, Isaac, and Jacob, and who is prominent in financial circles, or politics, will change his name to get away from God, even as Jonah fled from God.

The Jewish name of Karl Marx was Mordecai; Leon Trotsky's Jewish name was Bronstein; Litvinoff's original name was Finkelstein; and we could continue to Stalin, and name many others who would be recognized as world political figures, yet few would know that they were Jewish. They have changed their names. We could go to our own government during the last several administrations, and running down through the presidents' cabinets and the various departments of the bureaucracy, we can observe that a significant number of those in positions of leadership are of Jewish racial ancestry. Many of them will have American names because they, their father, or their grandfather, changed their Hebrew family name. But a Jew by any other name is still a Jew.

Because God has imparted special knowledge and abilities to the Jewish race, Satan has always sought to use the Jew to promote his own scheme to take over the world and elevate his throne above the throne of God (Isaiah 14:12–17). The devil used Ahab, Judas, and many others. The devil used an apostate Christian and an apostate Jew to write the Koran, a complete perversion of the Holy Scriptures, and start a false and militant religion among the seed of Abraham through Ishmael. The devil again used the most brilliant Jews of Europe, in these latter days, to launch a cruel political system that has murdered millions of Christians and practically eradicated the church from the entire continent of Asia.

Of course, we have to be careful and make a difference. God committed to Israel His laws. All the men who wrote the Bible were Israelites. Jesus Christ was an Israelite according to the flesh, from the lineage of David, born in Bethlehem of Judea. Of the twelve apostles, Satan was able to subvert and use only one of them. God's plan and purpose for this earth includes Israel as the head of all nations. This is why the Jews are back in the land of Palestine today.

God's covenant with Abraham included a protective clause: "And I will bless them that bless thee, and curse him that curseth thee . . ." (Genesis 12:3). Notice that the curse of God is against "him" (singular) who persecutes the seed of Abraham. The official position of our ministry has always been: If the Jews need to be punished, then God will do it. Many men have made a shipwreck of their ministry by taking it upon themselves to add to God's judgment of Israel.

At one time, the richest man in the world (or the second richest man, depending upon which financial source was accepted) approached Dr. E. F. Webber, founder of Southwest Radio Church. This wealthy individual was doubtless a good man and a solid church member. He offered to underwrite all the radio bills and greatly expand the radio ministry. There was just one condition: the message would have to be altered to exclude any mention of Israel being in a favored position with God. Naturally, Dr. Webber did not accept the offer.

Not long ago we had a good friend, and we still count him our friend, who had a tremendous work. We had a very close relationship from the beginning of his own special ministry. His work expanded from coast to coast in several communications media. But one day a few years ago, the first of a series of what we termed to be anti-Semitic articles appeared in his publication. I met with him and warned him of the sure consequences of the strange turn his work had taken, if he persisted in it. He did, and the sure consequences came. He lost every facet of his work. His health failed, and today when we mention his name, few people even remember him. He fell into Satan's trap. A trap has also been set in Jerusalem, and the Word of God declares in Zechariah 14:2, "... I will gather all nations against Jerusalem to battle...." The result is given in Zechariah 12:8–9: "In that day shall the LORD defend the inhabitants of Jerusalem.... And it shall come to pass in that day, that I will seek to destroy all the nations that come against Jerusalem."

In that day, the Antichrist, a Jew and an agent of Satan, will claim to be the real Messiah, and he will bring the armies of all nations to Israel to meet Jesus Christ returning to earth with the armies of Heaven. We are not told his real Hebrew name in the Bible, but Jesus said he would come to Israel in his own name, and the majority will receive him as the promised savior. But this will be the last time that Satan will be able to use a Jew for his own wicked and evil purposes.

The Antichrist will come in his own name, and not with a gentile alias, because he will have to establish his own Jewish identity to be an heir to the throne of David. His name, we are told in Revelation 13, will add up to 666, probably according to the Hebrew alphabet. His biblical name, the Antichrist, means that he will be against everything that Jesus Christ came to bring to mankind: hope, salvation, and eternal life. The comparison between Christ and Antichrist is as follows:

Christ	Antichrist
Christ came from Heaven.	Antichrist will come from the abyss.
Christ came to exalt the Father.	Antichrist will exalt himself.
Christ came to do the Father's will.	Antichrist will do Satan's will.

Christ	Antichrist
Christ glorified the Father on earth.	Antichrist will blaspheme the Name of God.
Christ was the Good Shepherd.	Antichrist will be the idle shepherd who will scatter the flock.
Christ was a man of sorrows.	Antichrist will be a king of fierce countenance.
Christ came to save the world.	Antichrist will try to destroy the world.
Christ was meek and lowly.	Antichrist will magnify himself above all that is of God.
Christ is the Prince of Peace.	Antichrist will be the desolator.
Christ is the firstfruits of resurrection.	Antichrist will be the firstborn of the eternal dead.
Christ is the way, the truth and the life.	Antichrist will be a liar and the way of death to millions.

What's in a name? Much . . . very much! Acts 4:10, 12 says: "Be it known unto you all . . . Jesus Christ of Nazareth, whom ye crucified . . . God raised from the dead. . . . Neither is there salvation in any other: for there is none other **name** under heaven given among men, whereby we must be saved."

What's In the Number 666 ?

The Apostle Paul wrote of the future world dictator who will rule over all nations during the coming Tribulation period: ". . . that man of sin . . . the son of perdition; Who opposeth and exalteth himself above all that is called God, or that is worshipped; so that he as God sitteth in the temple of God, shewing himself that he is God" (2 Thessalonians 2:3–4).

While many ecclesiastics today refute the notion of a personal Antichrist, by reading the chapter on Antichrist in the *Dictionary of Early Christian Beliefs* by Bercot we find that Justin Martyr, Clement of Anesandria, Origen, Iranaeus, Hippolytus, Tertullian, and others of the earliest Christian pastors and theologians believed in the biblical, personal Antichrist who would:

1. Be Satan incarnate.
2. Reign over all nations in the seven-year Tribulation.
3. Kill the two witnesses of God.
4. Kill everyone who will not take his mark or number.
5. Kill everyone who will not worship him as God.
6. Desolate the world.
7. His name in the Hebrew, Roman, or Greek number system will add up to 666.
8. He will be destroyed by Jesus Christ at His Second Coming.

The early church fathers may not have agreed entirely from which nation, race, or religion the Antichrist would come, but they agreed on the biblical warning about this coming man of sin. While many prominent political and religious personalities have had a name that added up to 666 in one of the language numerical structures, not one has had all the biblical qualifications—as yet.

We read of the Antichrist in Revelation 13:15–18 (thirteen is the number of sin and rebellion):

> And he had power to give life unto the image of the beast, that the image of the beast should both speak, and cause

that as many as would not worship the image of the beast should be killed. And he causeth all, both small and great, rich and poor, free and bond, to receive a mark in their right hand, or in their foreheads: And that no man might buy or sell, save he that had the mark, or the name of the beast, or the number of his name. Here is wisdom. Let him that hath understanding count the number of the beast: for it is the number of a man; and his number is Six hundred threescore and six.

Six is the number of man:
>Man was created on the sixth day.

Man's time is measured by:
>Sixty seconds in a minute (10 × 6).
>Sixty minutes in an hour (10 × 6).
>Twenty-four hours in a day (4 × 6).
>Twelve months in a year (2 × 6).

Man has:
>Six days a week to work.
>Six quarts of blood.
>Normal height is six feet.
>Average birth weight is six pounds.
>When he dies he is buried six feet under.

The number 666 indicates a claim to human perfection, but it also indicates a trinity of evil: False Prophet, Antichrist, and Satan. Although we are told that no one will know the exact date of Christ's return, there is no indication that we cannot know that the Antichrist is in the world. Jesus told John that the number of his name would tell us who he is. Many Bible scholars believe that the Antichrist will appear out of the revived Roman Empire. The Roman alphabetical numbering system was:

I	=	1
V	=	5
X	=	10
L	=	50
C	=	100
D	=	500
Total		666

By ignoring all other letters in names, many have identified certain popes as having a name adding up to 666. Martin Luther said that a pope would be the Antichrist. Others have come up with 666 in the names of politicians and world personalities.

As far as the mark of the beast is concerned, modern technology makes it not only possible, but also desirable. Increasing world terrorism now demands universal and personal identification. Computer chips began to be placed in animals in the 1970s, along with the arrival of computer code markings on products. In March 2002, a family in Florida—as reported in *Time* magazine—volunteered to become the first computer chip-implanted family. They were referred to as the Chipsons.

With an increasing number of nations obtaining nuclear weapons, the world is looking for a solution to prevent human extermination. The Antichrist could promise a seemingly reasonable solution and be given the reins to world government by the United Nations. Regardless of how he comes to power, he will commit the Abomination of Desolation, referred to four times in Daniel, twice by Jesus, twice by Paul, and by John in Revelation 13. The "abomination" is his standing in the Temple Mount declaring himself to the world as God. The "desolation" of the nations of the world follows. Egypt will be desolated so that no living thing will live on the land for forty years, and Egypt will be in the middle of the other nations desolated (Ezekiel 29).

Is the Antichrist in the world today? He could be. There is nothing unscriptural against putting a pencil to the numbers in his name.

666 and Counting

The number six is, without doubt, the number of man. Man was created on the sixth day, and the Creator ordained that man should work six days out of seven. Seven is the perfect number of God, and we read in Romans 3:23, "... all have sinned, and come short of the glory of God." Therefore, apart from God and in the flesh, man is bound with the number six—one short of the standard which God demands. Regardless of how many sixes man adds to his number, even to 666, six can never become seven, yet man in his own pride keeps trying.

The number of Antichrist—who will seek to become God—will be 666: "Here is wisdom. Let him that hath understanding count the number of the beast: for it is the number of a man; and his number is Six hundred threescore and six" (Revelation 13:18).

The first man to be born of natural parents, Cain, became a representative rebel. Eve thought she had gotten a man from the Lord, the promise of Genesis 3:15, the Redeemer who would bruise the serpent who deceived her. Cain was a bitter disappointment, because the Scriptures record that he was not of the Lord, but of the devil. (1 John 3:12). He was the first murderer, and he did six things to forever separate him from God:

1. He offered up a polluted sacrifice.
2. He murdered his brother.
3. He lied when confronted by God with his sin.
4. He received a mark (although for his own protection in the flesh, it was the mark of an unrepentant rebel).
5. He departed from God to go his own way.
6. He built a city rather than by faith looking for the city whose builder and maker is God.

The biblical number six always brands the man who defies God and God's anointed. Three prominent examples stand out in the Scriptures:

1. **Goliath.** This giant was six cubits in height; he had six pieces of armour; his spear head weighed six hundred shekels of iron.
2. **Nebuchadnezzar.** His image was sixty cubits high, six cubits broad, and the music played when everyone was supposed to fall down and worship the image was produced by a band playing six instruments.
3. **Solomon.** After God had made him the wisest and richest man in all the world, he began to get visions of divinity.

Not long ago we noticed the unusual patterns of the personal pronouns "I," "me," "my," and "mine" woven throughout the Book of Ecclesiastes that Solomon wrote. For example, in chapter two of Ecclesiastes, Solomon presented a roster of all his own accomplishments in life, giving no credit to God at all, and the four personal pronouns "I," "me," "my," and "mine" are used over sixty times.

The Assyrian Empire endured for 666 years before it was conquered by Babylon. Jerusalem was trodden down by the Roman Empire from the battle of Actium in 31 B.C. to the Saracen conquest in A.D. 636—666 years.

The number six is also imprinted on religion, because religion is the effort of man to save himself and become his own god. Religion says to man, "Do it for yourself." Christianity is accepting what God has already done through Jesus Christ. Quoting from *Number In Scripture* by E. W. Bullinger:

> ... 666 was the secret symbol of the ancient pagan mysteries connected with the worship of the Devil. It is today the secret connecting link between these ancient mysteries and their modern revival in Spiritualism, Theosophy, etc. The efforts of the great enemy are now directed toward uniting all into one whole. The newspapers, worldly and religious, are full of schemes for such a union. Reunion is in the air. The societies for the reunion of Christendom, and the conferences for the reunion of the churches, are alike part of the same great movement, and are all making for, and are signs of, the coming apostasy. During this age, separation is God's word for His people, and the mark of Christ; while union and reunion is the mark of Antichrist.

Dr. Bullinger gave the preceding warning against ecumenical efforts to bring the visible churches and denominations under one ecclesiastical structure in 1920. He also understood that apostate Christendom would become the church of Antichrist.

We have already mentioned that ancient Rome was in possession of Jerusalem—the city chosen by God to be the capital city of the earth—for 666 years. The publication of the Common Market, formerly *European Community,* now *Europe,* carried the following observation by the editor: "The EEC Rome Treaty supports . . . interpretations of the Books of Ezekiel, Daniel and Revelation that this 'Last Days' kingdom is a new Roman Empire."

It is indeed amazing that the Common Market's own publication admitted the similarity between the EEC alliance and the revived Roman Empire predicted for the end of the age in the Bible. Rome had its own peculiar numbering system. While the Greeks and Hebrews used their entire alphabets in numbering (for example, the first letter was one, the second letter was two, etc.), the Romans used only six letters in their alphabet for numbering purposes. Quoting from *Webster's Dictionary:* "Roman Numerals: the Roman letters used as numerals until the 10th century A.D.: In Roman numerals, I equals one, V equals five, X equals ten, L equals fifty, C equals one hundred, D equals five hundred."

The dictionary gives an additional number, M, which equals one thousand, but the letter M was added several centuries after the time of Christ, according to chronological sources, when the need for larger numbers arose. In the first centuries the need for a number as large as one thousand in finances and government was so rare they would simply add another D or two. Today, of course, if the Roman numerals were still being used, even their revised form, our own government would have to write the letter M over one trillion times to state the national debt. But in the first century, when the books of the New Testament were written, only six letters were used by the Romans in numbering, and it is no coincidence that the total value of these six letters is 666. This further emphasizes the fact of prophecy that the Antichrist will come out of the revived Roman Empire.

Many Bible scholars in the past have contended that the pope of the Roman Catholic Church will be Antichrist, and one of the foremost of such accusers was Martin Luther. This particular and questionable claim to honor for his holiness is supported by a subsequent discovery that the lettering on his pontifical bonnet in Latin, designating him as God's representative on earth, adds up to 666 according to the old Roman numbering system. However, in checking this claim out, our investigation indicated that this is only one of the many items of headgear that the pontiff may wear during the course of his duties.

Another interesting factor concerning the reign of Antichrist is that the Scriptures declare that he will establish his church, or tabernacle, in Jerusalem (Daniel 11:45). The Roman Catholic Church has never to this date recognized Israel as a nation, nor has the Vatican recognized Jerusalem as a part of Israel. The reason for this snobbery of Israel by the Catholic Church is that the Vatican considers the pope to be God's representative on earth to bring in His Kingdom. Inasmuch as the Bible designates Jerusalem as the center of God's Kingdom on earth, the Roman Catholic Church believes Jerusalem belongs to the pope. The Roman Catholic Church owns many properties in Israel, including dozens of churches. Even the Church of All Nations at the Garden of Gethsemane is really a "Roman Catholic" Church of All Nations.

In the month preceding the Yom Kippur War in October 1973, News France reported that former secretary of state

Henry Kissinger had worked out a six-point plan with King Faisal of Saudi Arabia for bringing lasting peace to the Middle East. One of the points in the peace plan was moving the Vatican to Jerusalem and giving the pope religious authority over the city. The December 1974 edition of *Christian Victory* gave credence to the Kissinger–Pope Paul arrangement in the article "Vatican May Move." The June-July issue of the *Biblical Research Monthly* published a letter received from a resident of Rome. It contains some interesting information:

> ... One of Italy's most trustworthy magazines carried this news item a few weeks ago: The Holy See has not only decided to fight to the finish to see the city of Jerusalem internationalized, but once its plan is accomplished, it intends to transfer the Apostolic See to the Holy City.... The last three popes: Pius XII, John XXII, Paul VI have been working for 25 years at the project of having Jerusalem declared an international territory, under the sole administration of the U.N. ... Although the Vatican official did admit that if Jerusalem were internationalized, probably all the political offices of the Vatican would be transferred there, the Pope might continue to live in Rome.

A UPI news release from the Vatican dated September 24, 1975, stated in part: "The report appeared in today's edition of the *Naples Daily Roma,* along with a photograph of a plastic model of a building resembling Notre Dame Cathedral in Paris which the newspaper said had been designed as the Jerusalem Vatican.... The newspaper said the move was under consideration [after] ... the next national elections...."

This is not to state, or even imply, any disrespect for the pope or the Catholic Church, but simply to report religious news that can be obtained from almost any secular news source. But it is exciting to live in these momentous days when Bible prophecy for the last days is coming alive before our very eyes.

There's a Number in Your Future

Everywhere we look today, government and finances are telling every man and woman that there is a number in their future. According to an edition of former Congressman Norrick's publication, the government is in the process of spending three billion dollars to set up a numbering system for all Americans. We would assume that the numbering system referred to by Mr. Norrick involves the new passport that is to be issued for all American citizens. Frances G. Knight, director of the Passport Office, who heads the project and who worked in the old NRA New Deal program, was interviewed in the March 3, 1975, edition of *U.S. News & World Report:*

> QUESTION: Would this involve the issuance of an identity card—with fingerprints to every citizen?
> ANSWER: In due course, yes.

An article that appeared in the October 25, 1982, edition of the *Times Union,* Rochester, New York, "All-Purpose Number Would Simplify Life" says in part: "The government is toying with the idea of giving us all numbers. If the legislation passes, we'll all have to carry national identity cards."

A nationally-known editorial writer, William Safire, wrote

the following editorial which appeared on September 9, 1982, in the *New York Times:*

> In a well-meaning effort to curb the employment of illegal aliens, and with the hearty good wishes of editorialists who ordinarily pride themselves on guarding against the intrusion of government into the private lives of individual Americans, Congress is about to take this generation's longest step toward totalitarianism. The first step downward on the Simpson staircase to "Big Brotherdom" is the requirement that within three years the federal government come up with a "secure system to determine employment eligibility in the United States." Despite denials, that means a national identity card. Nobody who is pushing the bill admits that—on the contrary, all sorts of "safeguards" and rhetorical warnings about not having to carry an identity card on one's person at all times are festooned on the bill. Much is made of the use of passports, social security cards, and driver's licenses as "preferred" forms of identification, but anyone who takes the trouble to read this legislation can see that the disclaimers are intended to help the medicine go down.
>
> Most American citizens are being led to believe that only aliens will be required to show "papers." But how can a prospective employer tell who is an alien? If the applicant could say, "I'm an American, I don't have any card," the new control system would immediately break down. The very basis of the proposed law is the notion that individuals must carry verifiable papers—more likely a card keyed to a "new government data bank"—to prove eligibility for work. . . .

Most Americans see no danger at all in a national identity card.

Most people even like the idea of a piece of plastic that tells the world, and themselves, who they are, "I'm me," says the little card. "I'm entitled to all the benefits that go with being provably and demonstrably me." Good citizens—the ones who vote regularly and who don't get into auto accidents might get a gold card. Once the down staircase is set in place, the temptation to take each next step will be irresistible. Certainly every business would want to ask customers to insert their identity cards into the whizbang credit checker. Banks, phone companies, schools, and hotels would all take advantage of the obvious utility of the document that could not be counterfeited. Law enforcement and tax collection would surely be easier because the federal government would know at all times exactly where everybody was and what they were spending.... We are entering the computer age. Combined with a national identity card—an abuse of power that Peter Rodino professes to oppose in the house, as he makes it inevitable—government computers and data banks pose a threat to personal liberty. Though aimed against "undocumented workers," the computer tattoo will be pressed on you and me.

It becomes more obvious every day that the European Union and the United States are working together in planning for the economic and political future.

It becomes apparent now that the American passport system will work co-jointly with a new European passport system, announced in the January-February 1976 edition of the former *European Community* magazine, now *Europe:*

> The European Community's . . . member countries have decided to replace national passports with a single type of European passport . . . as the first step toward a passport union. Once this union has been completed, citizens . . . will be able to travel from one end of the Community to the other without passing through customs. For Americans, it will mean a single customs check on entering the first EC country visited, and one on leaving. . . .

World population did not reach one billion until A.D. 1820. In less than two hundred years it has now reached almost eight billion. With millions of international travelers every year; an increasing emigration problem; plus trying to protect nations from international terrorism; and keeping track of the millions of Marys, Johns, Ivans, Chins, Baracks, etc., that international computerized number identification system is very near. Necessity will dictate control.

On the streets of our cities today we see international signs. Our children are learning the international metric system in school. Soon, there will be an international money system—Special Drawing Rights. International computer networks are being built to handle international trade, commerce, and travel. Numbers become more and more important, and as we have brought out in previous divisions of this study, authorities are predicting that before long everyone will be just a number in the computer. What will be the code number to the central computer? Of necessity, there will have to be one. Will it be 666?

The chief proponent of world government today was Dr. Henry Kissinger, and because he is a Jew from West Germany, a great peacemaker by reputation, called a man of wonder by heads of state, and married to a gentile, many have noted the similarity between many of the qualifications possessed by our former secretary of state which match those of the coming world ruler. Someone even worked out a numbering system for Dr. Kissinger's name. By giving the first letter "A" in our alphabet a value of six, and then by increasing the value of each subsequent letter by six, the numerical value of "KISSINGER" totals 666.

Just as Henry Kissinger, in retrospect, was a type of world personality that could be identified with the coming Antichrist, with his appearance upon the world scene a type of the coming mark of the beast also appeared. This instant buying with a common exchange medium other than currency in any nation of the world became known as the "credit card." The most universally accepted credit card is Visa, and Visa envisions being the leader in the coming cashless society. We quote from the October 17, 1983, edition of *U.S.A. Today*, from an article entitled "Visa Tests Credit Card of Future":

> Some 50,000 Ohioans today begin using a prototype of the "charge card of the future." The electron card, the key to Visa International's plan for a worldwide all-electronic payment system, is being introduced through four BancOne Corp. banks in the Ohio towns of Middletown, Milford, Sidney and Wapakoneth. Initially the card will be used only in automated teller machines, replacing the ATM card customers now use. Later this year BancOne customers also will use

the card instead of cash or checks in local retail stores. Ultimately, their checking or savings accounts will be debited electronically—eliminating paper transactions. Visa's plan is that banks worldwide eventually will replace their ATM cards or regular Visa credit cards with the "all-in-one" electron card.

According to the March 21, 1995, edition of the *New York Times*, plans were announced by Visa to put a microchip in each Visa credit card. This may cause us to wonder that if now every credit card may not have an implanted microchip.

Visa, as its name implies, is an international credit card system. It is perhaps the most used credit card. In 2009, according to statistics reported in Wikipedia, Visa's global network processed 62 billion transactions amounting to $4.4 trillion. In practically a flip of a switch, Visa could be changed to a system whereby no one in the world could buy or sell without a Visa credit card. With another flip of the switch, the Visa system could become a universal economic system as described in Revelation as the mark of the beast.

A rather vivid story about the stark reality of nature was related by a visitor to Niagara Falls. As the observer looked down into the roaring chasm, he glanced up the river and saw what appeared to be a large bird on one of the many chunks of ice floating rapidly toward the falls. As the piece of ice carrying the bird came nearer, the man noticed that it was a huge eagle feeding on a dead sheep. Evidently the lamb had tried to go out on the ice to get a drink of water, and the ice broke off. In the zero temperature, with water splashing over the small iceberg, the sheep froze to death. As the man watched, the eagle continued to feed on the animal until the ice carrying it was only a few hundred feet from the roaring cataract. The eagle was in no great hurry to leave off from stuffing itself, because with one giant sweep of its wings, it could lift up and fly away even as the carcass of the sheep plunged over the falls. About a hundred feet from the edge, the eagle decided to leave a certain margin for safety, and it spread its powerful wings to fly away. As the visitor turned to look once again at the awesome spectacle below, his ears were pierced by the eagle's terrified scream. The poor creature had waited too long. The water spray had iced its feet to the fleece of the sheep, and it plunged to destruction.

This tragic but true story of nature has a vital application for the world today. Many people know that a catastrophe of world proportions is approaching. They also know that the only way of escape is by receiving Jesus Christ, the only Savior from sin. But yet they linger over the delights of this rotting world system and put off the most important and far-reaching decision they will ever make. Christ could come at any time to "catch up" His children. Then it will be too late to escape the agonies of the seven-year period of Tribulation.

Yes, you may receive Christ and be saved after the Rapture. But severe persecution, economic deprivation, and a martyr's death await the vast majority of those who are faithful to Christ during this time. This book is dedicated to those who, like the poor eagle, will wait a bit too long to seek deliverance and shall find themselves swept over the precipice into a stage of history that Jesus described as "... great tribulation, such as was not since the beginning of the world to this time, no, nor ever shall be" (Matthew 24:21).

We pray that you, the reader, will not be numbered among those who waited too long and who must pass through the cataclysmic judgments of the Great Tribulation. Acknowledge before God that you are a sinner and ask Christ to forgive you and grant you eternal life. Claim the wonderful promise that is found in John 1:12: "But as many as received him, to them gave he power [authority] to become the sons of God. . . ." May God help you to make that decision right now. You have a choice to make. We hope it will be the right choice.

Chapter 12

What Does 666 Mean to You?

Recently a dear saint called and asked for prayer concerning her health. Evidently she was suffering from many different kinds of aches, pains, and bodily malfunctions. She simply could not understand why God would allow her to suffer from all these plagues and illnesses. So I asked her about her age, and she responded that she was eighty. I explained to her that she had just told me what her problem was. She was eighty years old. According to our Bible, God has given us a seventy-year limited warranty.

I have no animosity against or affinity for the number eighty. However, being eighty-nine at the completion of this book, eighty to me meant more aches, pains, doctor bills, limited activities, and restrictions as in outreach and associations.

The number three hundred may be the distance to the next town, or what is left in my checking account. However the three hundredth day on my calendar means the days are beginning to get shorter; leaves on the trees are changing color; the daily temperature is getting cooler; and we have to begin making certain changes to get ready for the winter weather that will be arriving soon.

The number 666, without a context, is no more important or interesting than 333. However, within the prophetic context of the last days, its meaning is almost infinite. It means a world government under the authority of a mad dictator. It means a serious adjustment in economic, political, and moral attitudes and conduct in order to make the nations willing to accept the man of sin, called the Antichrist. Every rule and biblical precept applying to God's three ordained institutions must be reversed. Jesus said that as it was in the days of Noah and the days of Lot, so it must be in order for the Antichrist to be placed in charge of this world system.

In 1991, I attended the convention of National Religious Broadcasters in Washington, D.C. At the evening banquet, I sat next to Dr. Robert Lindsted, with whom I had cooperated many times on foreign missions. The main speaker was President George H. W. Bush. In his address he shared his vision of a new world order with the convention members, which I estimate to be approximately one thousand. Eight times in his speech the president referenced the creation of a new world order. When he mentioned it, all the delegates would immediately rise to their feet, clap, and cheer. That is, it seemed, every member except Dr. Lindsted and myself. He and I agreed that if a seemingly conservative president, and one thousand seemingly conservative Christian leaders were in favor of a new world order, then one must be in our immediate future.

There are many other changes that the number 666 implies. For example, I reference part of my letter to our constituency from July 2011:

In perusing the *2011 World Almanac* we find:

- In 1932, 13 out of 79 marriages ended in divorce.
- In 2010, 34 out of 66 marriages ended in divorce, more than half.
- In the past 16 years 80 million babies have been born.
- More than 50 percent of the 80 million were born out of wedlock.
- In the past 16 years there were 22 million recorded abortions.
- In 1962 it became illegal to pray or read the Bible in public schools.
- It is now illegal to openly criticize or disagree with the homosexual lifestyle.
- President Obama declared June to be homosexual pride month.
- President Obama said that homosexuals are better than heterosexuals.
- President Obama has appointed over 150 homosexuals to high positions.
- In June 2011, the flag of Sodom (the rainbow flag) flew over the Federal Reserve; tomorrow, the White House?
- The U.S., under the blessing of God, is the richest nation the world has ever known, yet our money is supporting pagan nations around the world. We are hopelessly in debt and most of what we eat and wear is imported.
- We have an illegal alien problem that our government doesn't care enough about to solve.
- Our prisons are overcrowded and the inmates are mostly from one-parent homes.

In Israel God called men like Elijah and Jeremiah to warn

the nation of their sins and call for repentance. On two occasions kings Asa and Josiah tore down the bathhouses and chased the sodomites out of Jerusalem, and in turn God blessed Israel.

Concerning the depths of moral depravity that is now accepted as normal, if not preferable, moral conduct by the highest officials in the nation without protest from ninety-nine out of every one hundred pastors, we reference an article I wrote in our August 2011 *Prophetic Observer:*

One of the first official acts of Barack Obama upon becoming president of the United States was to issue a proclamation designating June, the traditional month of brides, as LGBT (or homosexual) Month. According to Obama this was done to honor this minority segment of the U.S. population (1.7 percent) as this nation's most important citizens. The full text of the proclamation was carried in the June 27, 2009, edition of *San Francisco Pride.* The reason for dedicating a month to honor homosexuals was stated in the opening sentence:

"LGBT [Lesbian, Gay, Bisexual, Transgender] Americans have made and continue to make great and lasting contributions that continue to strengthen the fabric of American society; LGBT Americans have mobilized the nation to respond to the domestic HIV/AIDS epidemic, and played a vital role in broadening the country's response in the HIV epidemic."

This opening statement regarding the actual role homosexuals have played in U.S. history and the president's appraisal of their alerting other citizens to the need of solving the AIDS curse on humanity is beyond rational comprehension. Obama's narcissistic mindset aims to change the truth into a lie and a lie into the truth. It is a known fact that AIDS was first recognized as a new disease in 1981, when a number of young gay men in New York and Los Angeles were diagnosed with symptoms not usually seen in individuals with healthy immune systems. Originally named GRIDS for Gay Related Immune Deficiency Syndrome, AIDS is mainly transmitted through sexual activity and has already caused the death of hundreds of millions of people worldwide....

"I am proud to be the first president to appoint LGBT candidates to Senate-confirmed positions in the first 100 days of an administration. These individuals embody the best qualities we seek in public service."

The fact is that the Senate complained that Obama was appointing "czars" without confirmation. The record also indicates that he has appointed over 150 homosexuals to high government offices with administrative responsibilities. It is difficult to name anyone in the new administration who is not a homosexual....

As to future plans for the homosexual segment of the population, the president continued:

"My administration has partnered with the LGBT community to advance a wide range of initiatives. At the international level, I have joined efforts at the United Nations to decriminalize homosexuality around the world.... These measures include supporting civil unions... ensuring adoption rights, and ending existing 'Don't Ask, Don't Tell' policies in a way that strengthens the armed forces and national security."

Mr. Obama admits, or professes, that he is not just a member of the Democratic Party, but he is also a member of the LGBT Party and that he will work to accomplish all homosexual goals while in office....

One of the goals of the Communist Party in weakening the United States was to use homosexuality, as stated in Agenda 21. One specific goal was to infiltrate the armed forces. This was started by Bill Clinton during his presidency through the "Don't Ask, Don't Tell" program under which 16,000 homosexuals enlisted. However some 12,000 had to be dismissed because they not only told, they did what homosexuals do.

President Obama got the bill passed to allow unrestricted enrollment in the military services for homosexuals by submitting a false report to a lame duck Congress. According to a June 27, 2011, report by World Net Daily, the presidential report to Congress stated that 70 percent of the military polled said it was all right with them for gays to enlist. According to the Inspector General, the White House wrote the report before any such poll was taken....

Another of the stated goals of the homosexual conspiracy is the destruction of the family unit. God made Adam first and then Eve, and the couple subsequently had two children, Cain and Abel. God established the family between one man and one woman. While this order may vary in some religions and cultures, all still maintain that the family begins with a man and a woman. Without family, no civilization, social order, or government can exist. Without this continuing relationship between the sexes, humanity degenerates to the level of animals. President Obama ordered that the Defense of Marriage Act not be defended by the federal government, and in a statement referenced by Yahoo! News on June 23, 2011, President Obama indicated he saw no difference between marriage of a man and a woman to the marriage of two of the same sex.

Seven states have made same-sex marriages legal, the latest being New York. Catholic bishop Dimmarzio stated in a June 30, 2011, *CNS* news item that the Christian marriage has been demonized by both Democrats and Republicans, that the pillar of civilization has been destroyed, and that no senator, congressman, or government representative be allowed to enter any Catholic church in his parish.

This nation of some 300 million does not yet realize what is happening. According to the Department of Defense budget report on July 7, 2011, the spending will increase greatly due to the Defense of Marriage Act being trashed and the president's acceptance of same-sex marriages because homosexual mates will now have the same rights to home expenses and support as Army wives.

A typical appointee of Obama is Chai Feldblum, a lesbian whom he selected to head the Equal Employment Commission. In fact, everyone who heads the federal employment agencies seems to be homosexual, according to the press recordings at the beginning of the president's term in 2009. According to the Traditional Values Coalition, Ms. (or whatever) Feldblum is not only a homosexual, she is polyamorous, meaning having more than one intimate relationship at a time with the knowledge and consent of everyone involved. Feldblum is a strong believer in gay-marriage rights. Chai is quoted as saying, "I'm having a hard time coming up with any case in which religious liberty should win. Gays win, Christians lose!" . . .

Obama's appointment of Kevin Jennings (founder of GLSEN [Gay, Lesbian, & Straight Education Network] and one of the most outspoken homosexual activists in the world) to head the Department of Education has now led to the demand that all schoolbooks include the history and lives of so-called famous homosexuals (Fox News, July 6, 2011). *CNS* reported a homosexual party sponsored by the Department of Education and Kathleen Sebelius, another Obama appointee, stated this party was to "insure that LGBT students' rights were protected." Now, many universities in the United States are granting LGBT degrees. A federal tax grant (your money) was given to the Gay Straight Alliance Network to teach homosexual youth to perform safer sex to keep the AIDS statistics down.

Many major government departments in Washington, D.C., now have inner homosexual departments with websites. When was our Constitution amended to allow separate inner subversive units, paid for by taxpayer's dollars, whose purpose so stated is to teach our children how to "safely" sodomize each other and close our churches? The Department of Justice has a homosexual department and website headed, "DOJ PRIDE—The Official Web Presence for LGBT Employees and Their Allies." The website is composed of eight pages on the mission and purpose for the Department of Justice, but summarizes it as follows:

"Besides conducting outreach to prospective employees, DOJ Pride sponsors brown-bag lectures featuring experts in the LGBT community discussing issues of importance in DOJ members, such as marriage equality. Finally, through its yearly Pride Month Celebration and Award Ceremony, DOJ Pride has taken an active role in recognizing the work of LGBT supporters inside the Department of Justice, the Federal Government, and the Nation."

Even the CIA is jumping on the pro-LGBT bandwagon. A news item dated July 11, 2011, on DallasCaller.com is headlined "CIA to Sponsor LGBT Advocacy Group Summit." The reason stated for this CIA diversion is "to promote diversity within CIA ranks," says CIA spokeswoman Marie Hart. Evidently, promoting homosexuality takes precedent above protecting our nation against terrorists and spies. The president and his offices have been bought by the homosexual conspiracy. As Oklahoma representative Sally Kern states repeatedly in her book *The Stoning of Sally Kern,* this is the greatest danger to the freedom and sovereignty of the United States in our nation today.

There are sixteen references in the books of the prophets to warn nations against committing the sins of Sodom and Gomorrah. Israel's two good kings, Asa and Josiah, began their reigns by trashing the sodomites' houses, probably bathhouses, and chasing them out of town. There are six references to Sodom and Gomorrah in the Gospels and Jesus was not exactly suggesting these cities as vacation resorts.

Paul began his letter to the Christians in Rome to warn them against becoming morally and spiritually corrupted by that homosexually-saturated society. [In Romans 1:26–28, 32], Paul warned the Christians about homosexuals who sin against God's created order....

When Peter wrote his last epistle he knew that within a few days he would be crucified, and he evidently felt he had to leave the warning to Christians that they must not follow the example of Sodom and Gomorrah (2 Peter 2:6). (I did not teach from the *Southern Baptist Quarterly* lesson for July 3, 2011, because it indicated that the sin Peter referenced was gluttony or over-eating.)

Jude, the half-brother of Jesus, was determined to write an epistle on the love of God in sending his brother Jesus to die for the sins of the world. However the Holy Spirit stopped him and told him to write to the churches warning about sodomites in the pulpit (Jude verses 4, 7–8)....

The Bible says that homosexuality is a sin, and the fear of homosexuality is a concern that every Christian should have. Today sodomites are being ordained as deacons and pastors in many churches.... Even Glenn Beck, Bill O'Reilly of Fox, or Rush Limbaugh, recognized voices for conservatism, dare not mention one negative word about homosexuals.

Our president has made a commitment to fulfill the homosexual agenda for the sodomization of the United States. He is being paid to do it. Pastors and teachers are scared to touch the subject, hiding in fear behind their pulpits. Over and over Sodom is given in the Bible as an example for nations who act likewise. It is up to Christians like me, an 89-year-old WWII veteran who spent three years in the South Pacific, to warn our nation that God is going to give up on us unless there is an awakening in our nation and repentance in our churches.

The Bible describes the homosexual lifestyle as "unseemly," meaning wicked beyond imagination. Yet the homosexuals among us do have the right to vote, own property, and engage in business with only ecclesiastical limitations, as should be understandable. They also have the right to live together and pursue their particular lifestyle. Yet this is not enough for our government, which is now trying to force the acceptance of this unhealthy, immoral, even deadly lifestyle on all of us. I love my country, so please join me in prayer to our God who hears when no one else does....

The three pillars upon which our civilization has endured—family, church, and government—is in a state of collapse and deterioration. The absurdity and incomprehensible idiocy of what is happening to our nation was illustrated in 2011 when the U.S. Health Department spent millions of the taxpayers' dollars to measure the private parts of homosexual males at the cost of $10,000 per measurement. The one question asked was, how were the statistics to be used. The prophet Daniel's reference to the Antichrist having no desire for women may have a relationship to what is happening worldwide.

Jesus said that in the last days there would be pestilences, meaning pandemic epidemics. The greatest plague the world has ever seen is now taking place before our very eyes, yet few citizens realize it. Anyone can check the Internet and from the World Health Organization statistics find that 59 percent of the populations of some nations in Africa have HIV or AIDS, and it is spreading rapidly to the other nations of the world. This international health problem, caused mainly by homosexuality, will eventually bankrupt the world. Newt Gingrich, in his book *Real Change,* reports that in just three counties in Florida, AIDS victims hit Medicare for $480 million dollars in just six months.

As I conclude the final revisions and additions to a book I last updated in 1987, a few of the headline news items on my desk explain to us the real meaning of 666 in the times in which we live. They are as follows:

- **2011 Worst Year Ever for U.S Disasters**
- **Germany—Christian Parents Jailed for Keeping Children From Sex Education Classes**
- **Marriage Couples Set a New Record Low**
- **Girl Scouts Disbanded for Not Allowing Transgenders**
- **Christian Clubs Not Allowed in Colleges**
- **74% Say Martin Luther King Is Better Than Jesus**
- **Bibles Banned in Military Hospital**
- **Climate Change the Worst Scandal of Our Time**
- **Britain—Islam In, Christianity Out**
- **Blair and Warren Propose a Common World Faith**
- **Gay History Taught in California Schools**
- **D.C. Considers Same-Sex Divorce Bill**
- **Senate Legalizes Sodomy and Bestiality in Military Services**
- **Nuclear Fission Storms on Sun Slam Earth**

What the world news reports tell us is that in the once-Christian western world, the Christian faith is increasingly being legally restricted These are the beginnings of the time of 666 when anyone who names the name of Jesus Christ and refuses to take the mark of the beast will be beheaded.

To many this may seem farfetched, but many of the things happening today were farfetched ten years ago. The number 666 is not just a number, it is a satanic program that soon will bring all nations to worshipping the image of the Antichrist on television. This could only happen in our time.

Every political ideology, every religious trend, economic reality, and scientific possibility is in evidence today. But is the Antichrist alive and in the world today?

We encourage the reader to keep abreast of the prophetic signs of our time in view of world events that are rapidly moving us to the day foretold in Revelation 13. Pray and be ready for the coming of the Lord.

Is the Antichrist Alive Today?

Jesus Christ warned that in the very last days many false christs and false prophets would appear, and if possible, deceive the very elect. Within the context of 1 John 2:18, the pre-appearance of many types of antichrist would signal the very last times, the period of time preceding the literal return of Jesus Christ. However, four times in John's first and second epistles, there are references to types of antichrist that look forward to the Antichrist, a real person to appear in the last days.

The Apostle John, while a prisoner on the isle of Patmos, favored us with more specific information about this prophetic personality, the Antichrist. According to John's description of this world dictator in Revelation 13, and other scriptures, the Antichrist is to be a supreme world dictator. He will be given this authority by an alliance of ten nations, or ten alliances of nations. When this occurs, then the Antichrist will have control over all money, all business, all international military forces, and all religions. Anyone who does not take his mark and number will be killed by beheading, and the same fate would befall any person on earth who did not acknowledge and worship him as their god. In some twenty-five or more places in the Book of Revelation he is referred to as "the beast."

As prophesied, in the twentieth century three strong types of Antichrist appeared:

1. Hitler of Germany, who was worshipped as a god, killed over 6 million Jews, and started WWII in which 35 million died.
2. Stalin of Russia, who envisioned a communist world in which he would be the supreme dictator, killed an estimated 100 million.
3. Mao Tse-Tung of China, like Stalin, persecuted Christians, closed churches, and killed an estimated 100 million.

All three had absolute authority over their individual nation, but not over the entire world.

We must wonder what world conditions will occur that would dictate giving this one-world dictator, called the beast, absolute authority over the entire world. One reason, of course, would be the fear of a universally devastating nuclear war. The United Nations was founded at the close of World War II to form a united world forum to prevent future wars. It has failed miserably in its purpose. As Jesus prophesied, wars and rumors of wars have continued, and now eight nations have enough atomic weapons to destroy the world a thousand times over, and the spread of such weapons continues. Iran's stated purpose of developing nuclear weapons is to create a worldwide inferno to bring their so-called spiritual champion, the Mahdi, to kill everyone who is not a Muslim.

If there is one nation, or one man of prominence, who could convince the nations that such a world catastrophe could be avoided by turning all the nuclear weapons over to him, he could rule the world. Would this person be the head of the United Nations, or a coalition of nations? Probably. This could also mean that the Antichrist is alive today.

World Population Control

Some fifty-eight years after God created the first man and woman and commanded they be fruitful in having sons and daughters, the world's population reached one billion souls in 1820. In less than just two hundred years, the world population has increased to more than seven billion. While we are still in fairly good shape here in the United States, where we have a population of one-third of a billion, there are serious concerns about how the expanding billions are going to be taken care of when there are already serious problems in many nations of the world.

Under a massive international population control program, new contraceptive methods have been advertised, produced, and used, but the population has continued to increase. Next, massive abortion programs of ending life in the womb—without calling it murder—have been instituted. According to statistics on page 175 of the *2011 World Almanac,* in the United States alone, between 1970 and 2006, there were over one and a half million abortions performed. It is conservative to estimate in just the United States, in the last forty years, at least fifty million babies have been aborted. Without the international abortion programs, the present world population would probably be about ten billion.

Another important part of the world population control program has been the world promotion of homosexuality. Men having sex with men, and women having sex with women, do not produce babies.

U.S. President Barack Obama, immediately after he took the oath of office, issued a presidential directive making June—the month of brides—Gay Pride Month, and states that homosexuals (LGBTs) are the best people we have in the United States. In the first hundred days of his term in office, he was appointing them to high positions in his administration. As far as I can determine, the head of every important department in our national government is filled by a homosexual. The head of the Department of Education has been Mr. Jennings, a world noted homosexual activist. The Department of Education receives more than $20 billion a month to spend. Schools are now being used to promote the homosexual lifestyle as a preferred lifestyle. Almost every major college now offers LGBT classes and degrees. Christian-based groups like the Boy Scouts and Girl Scouts are having to disband because they will not knowingly enroll homosexuals. State departments of education are passing laws like SB-48 of California, which requires schoolbooks to praise and commend the homosexual lifestyle. These laws are worded and passed to make homosexuals out of the younger generation.

Also, as widely reported, Mr. Obama has removed government recognition of the Defense of Marriage Act, indicating his preference that men and women do not now marry and have children. A OneNewsNow item dated December 21, 2011, stated in part: "A pro-family activist says a U.S. Department of Justice lawyer's arguments against the Defense of Marriage

Act further enforces the Obama administration's desire for support from the homosexual lobby."

A news story by the *Washington Post* on December 15, 2011, was headed: **"Married Couples at a New Low."**

The story related that 50 percent of teenagers now say they do not intend to get married, which indicates a disastrous destruction of the family unit established by God—the foundation of order, church, government, and law. A *Christian Post* news item of December 28, 2011, was headed, "Obama Sends Letter of Congratulations to Gay Married Couple." Our own secretary of state, Hillary Clinton, is also an entertaining agent for international gay parades, and numerous articles from Israel report an increasing homosexual population in Israel. Scores of other news items relating to the decline of the family, and the increase in local, national, and international homosexual activity and relationships are pictured on the society pages of newspapers depicting homosexual marriages. Daniel prophesied that the Antichrist would not regard the desire of women, which could mean he will be a homosexual.

According to Bible chronology, seven years before Jesus Christ returns literally to this planet and presents Himself to Israel as King of Kings and Lord of Lords, the Antichrist must appear and demand that everyone in the world worship him as God. Jesus also said of world conditions that when this happens, it would be as it was in the days of Lot.

According to 3 Ussher, on a day in 1897 B.C., God destroyed Sodom and Gomorrah, as confirmed in the Bible, in a fiery judgment for the sin of homosexuality. The explosion left a hole in the ground thirteen hundred feet deep and forty miles long. It is known today as the Dead Sea, in which nothing lives. According to the prophetic Word, the world will again be like it was in Sodom when the Antichrist appears. Therefore, it seems logical that the Antichrist is alive today.

Computer Economics

We read in Revelation 13 that under the Antichrist's economic system, no person in all the world will be able to buy even a loaf of bread or sell a pig with money. Every individual in every country in the world must have a number issued by the world government and have a mark, perhaps a computer chip, in their right hand or on their forehead. It seems obvious that a world government must have a universal exchange system.

The first computer I saw, or even heard of, was in 1943 when the Army sent our unit four new radar systems. On the back of each one was a large unit about the size of a piano on wheels. When I asked what that was, I was told it was a computer.

The first thing a dictator or political system like communism does in taking over a nation and controlling the population is take charge of the monetary exchange system. This will be true of the Antichrist system. Often, the present money or exchange units are declared void and new money is issued. This is the first thing that Hitler, Stalin, and Mao did. Often, the current money or exchange system has to be destroyed gradually before the citizenry becomes dependent upon the government.

In 2008, with the election of Mr. Obama, the homeowners in our nation suddenly lost $7.35 trillion dollars in real estate value. When Bill Clinton was president he had laws passed where banks or savings institutions had to build homes for those who had no jobs or were not able to pay for them. The loans were called "subprime mortgages," which were really worthless paper. President Bush covered up this scam to prevent an economic collapse, but when Mr. Obama was elected, the cover was gone and millions of houses were dumped on the market. As a result, $7.35 trillion dollars worth of buying power was taken away from our nation's middle class. No wonder we had a depression.

This economic problem in the United States became part of a world economic problem. Most nations today are deeply in debt. There are tremendous fluctuations in the value of international currencies. There is a demand for a world currency based on "drawing rights," which could be controlled worldwide by computer transactions.

A headline in the *Financial Times* dated December 14, 2011, reads: **"Storm Clouds Darken Global Economy."**

Even the Catholic Church is demanding a world economic system. Another headline in the *New York Post,* dated December 8, 2011, reads: **"Euro's Fall May Doom All."**

Another headline from *Financial Times,* dated December 8, 2011, reads: **"The Terrible Consequences of a Eurozone Collapse."**

Whether by design or just bad economics or political blundering, the United States is trillions of dollars in debt to China and other nations. If the real truth was known, the one hundred dollar bill in your pocket might be worth a loaf of bread. In fact, in Revelation 6, it is indicated that during the Great Tribulation under the Antichrist, it will take a day's wages just to buy a loaf of bread.

Our politicians promise us that they will restore the happy

times of the Eisenhower, Ford, and Reagan administrations, but the real truth lies in two news headlines that crossed my desk recently: **"Obama Asks for Debt Hike Limit"** and **"120 K-Mart and Sears Stores Close."**

All of the collective international economic news indicates a coming one-world economic and monetary exchange system, based on drawing rights, and controlled by a massive central computer system. This international economic concern is being promoted today, and would indicate the Antichrist may be alive and is waiting to install his individual numbering system.

Pandemic Catastrophes

In Matthew 24 and Luke 21, Jesus said when He came the second time, He would come to a world beset with disease epidemics, earthquakes, and cosmic eruptions.

By checking the U.S. Geological Department website, it can be verified that earthquakes have increased in the United States from approximately twelve hundred in 1985 to thirty-three hundred in 2011. We have an average of fifty small earthquakes a year in Oklahoma, but in 2011 there have been over a thousand some of them approaching 6.0 on the Richter scale.

In the United States in 2011, there have been over 750 tornadoes, twice as many as normal, and they have been unusually destructive, killing hundreds of people and destroying entire cities, like Joplin, Missouri. Also in 2011, there have been unusually destructive floods on the Missouri and Mississippi rivers, but unusually severe droughts in Arizona, New Mexico, Kansas, Texas, and Oklahoma, where wheat farmers turned cattle on their fields because the wheat didn't mature due to no rain. The earthquake in Japan with the resulting tsunami was one of the worst in recorded history. Also in Oklahoma in 2011, there were over a thousand earthquakes. Although most were in the 3.0 to 4.0 range on the Richter scale, some were above the 5.0 strength, strong enough to do structural damage to some buildings.

The headlines on page one of MAIL Online for January 4, 2012, reads, **"2011 To Become Worst Ever Year for Disasters."**

A Fox News item dated December 28, 2011, read in part: "Sun Storms Slam Earth." Our sun is a medium-sized star, one million miles in diameter, a monstrous nuclear fusion object converting hydrogen to heat and light. Dying stars erupt out of nuclear control for a period of seven to fourteen days when the atoms are stripped of their shells, and the entire mass collapses into a ball approximately fifteen miles across where the gravity is so intense that even light cannot escape. It is then called a black hole, where nothing can escape forever. The black hole is also called a nova, and such novas are observed to occur in our own galaxy some thirty times a year. The current solar storms on our sun are due to reach a climax in 2013, which may be reason for concern. We read in Revelation 6:12 that in the coming Great Tribulation, the moon will become as blood and the sun will become black.

Another prophetic sign that we are living in the last days, and the Antichrist could be alive in the world today, is that international television will make it possible for everyone in every nation to worship the image of the Antichrist. The image of a person on television moves and speaks, as we are told the image of the Antichrist would. It will also be possible for all the world to see the bodies of God's two witnesses lying in the streets of Jerusalem, as we read in Revelation 11:9. Television makes possible the fulfillment of this most specific prophecy in the Bible.

We are informed in 2 Thessalonians 2 that in order for Satan's false messiah, the Antichrist, to receive world acceptance, God would send upon the nations a delusion that they will believe a lie. An example of how all the world can be deceived is the recent claim of the Obama administration that the climate is becoming warmer and warmer because of increasing CO_2 in the atmosphere. The *London Telegraph* in a lengthy article in the December 12, 2011, edition, in a bold headline reported: **"Climate Change, The Worst Scientific Scandal of Our Generation."**

An editorial in the *Washington Times* in the November 20, 2011, edition, under the heading, "A Climate of Fraud," indicated the climate change fraud to be the biggest lie ever perpetrated upon the human race.

With the continued proliferation of nuclear weapons, increasing populations, and increasing international catastrophes, including famines and diseases like AIDS (affecting over half the populations in some African nations), the need for a world savior like the false biblical Antichrist will increase. Many in the previous generation thought Henry Kissinger would be the Antichrist; more recently many proposed King Carlos of Spain; others today point to George Soros. Henry Kissinger thought President Obama would make a great president of planet Earth.

The context of scriptures relating to the Antichrist indicate that Christians—and the Holy Spirit—will be taken out of the world so that those remaining in the world will be deceived. Therefore, Christians today may never know who the Antichrist is. This we are assured of, as we read in 2 Thessalonians 2:8, the Antichrist and his government will be destroyed with the brightness of the Lord's coming.

"Even so, come, Lord Jesus" (Revelation 22:20).